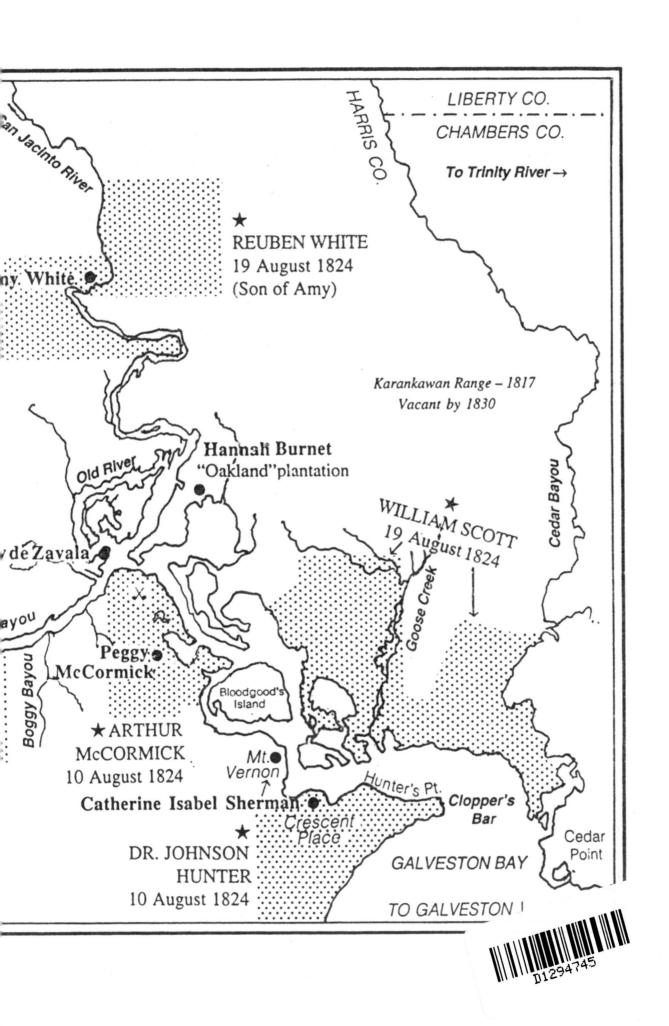

HARRIS CO.

LIBERTY CO.

CHAMBERS CO.

To Trinity River →

an Jacinto River

★
REUBEN WHITE
19 August 1824
(Son of Amy)

ny. White.

Karankawan Range – 1817
Vacant by 1830

Hannah Burnet
"Oakland" plantation

Old River

★
WILLIAM SCOTT
19 August 1824

Goose Creek

Cedar Bayou

de Zavala

ayou

Boggy Bayou

**Peggy
McCormick**

Bloodgood's
Island

★ **ARTHUR
McCORMICK**
10 August 1824

Mt.
Vernon

Catherine Isabel Sherman

Hunter's Pt.

Clopper's
Bar

Cedar
Point

★
DR. JOHNSON
HUNTER
10 August 1824

*Crescent
Place*

GALVESTON BAY

TO GALVESTON I

Best wishes,

Betty Trapp Chapman

Jan. 11, 2001

The extraordinary history of the city of Houston has now been told more thoroughly and vividly with the publication of *Houston Women: Invisible Threads in the Tapestry*. Bank United is pleased to have underwritten this project through the Houston Junior Forum in appreciation of the women featured on these pages, and the untold number of others, who have woven a colorful fabric of life that has made Houston a diversified, successful and vibrant American city. Houston has and continues to foster a spirit of independence in its women, men and industry. May we continue to benefit from this spirit, and may we learn from our incredible history as we add to its pages.

BANK UNITED

HOUSTON

Invisible Threads in the Tapestry

OPEN
VENINGS

WOMEN

By Betty Trapp Chapman

DEDICATION
For Laura and Elizabeth
Haley and Lindsey

Previous page: Although the official name of the group pictured here on the mezzanine balcony of the Rice Hotel is not known, its members are believed to have been engaged in raising money for a milk fund. It is quite likely that they provided milk for deprived children as part of their community service. (Story Sloane's Gallery)

The Donning Company Publishers

184 Business Park Drive, Suite 106

Virginia Beach, VA 23462

Steve Mull, General Manager

Barbara A. Bolton, Project Director

Diana Glynn, Project Research Coordinator

Dawn V. Kofroth, Assistant General Manager

Sally Clarke Davis, Editor

Lori Wiley, Graphic Designer

Scott Rule, Marketing Coordinator

John Harrell, Imaging Artist

Library of Congress Cataloging-in-Publication Data

TO COME

Printed in the United States of America

TABLE OF CONTENTS

FOREWORD

When George and I moved to Houston in 1959, I did not realize at the time that the move automatically made me a member of one of the most impressive and influential groups of people I would ever have the privilege of knowing: the women of Houston, Texas.

When you look at all of Houston's wonderful achievements—from our outstanding medical facilities to NASA, the oil industry to high tech, our sports teams and cultural opportunities—you will find both in front of and behind the scenes an incredible group of women who have shaped this great city from its very beginning.

When we first moved here, the women I got to know best were the stay-at-home moms who devoted themselves to their families and their communities. They were the PTA presidents, the hospital volunteers, the scorekeepers at the Little League games, the next-door neighbors who were there for each other in good times and bad. In many ways, they were the backbones of their communities—the strongest thread that made up the tapestry that was our city. They still are today.

As the years progressed and women everywhere started playing a more prominent role on the public stage, Houston women were once again among the strongest and the best. They became doctors, astronauts, lawyers, mayors, senators, firefighters, police officers, business owners, philanthropists, journalists—and yes, they were still PTA presidents, too. Going back to the pioneer days, these women have a fascinating story to tell—a story of courage and tenacity, triumph and achievement. Thanks to the Houston Junior Forum and Betty Trapp Chapman—incredible women all!—that story is finally told in this truly inspiring book, *Houston Women: Invisible Threads in the Tapestry*. It is a wonderful celebration of the women who helped make this great city the kind of place George and I are so privileged to call home.

Barbara Bush

(Houston Metropolitan Research Center, Houston Public Library)

ACKNOWLEDGMENTS

To the many who helped me along the way as I have worked on this book, I am indebted. Foremost is The Heritage Society, who over twenty years ago sparked my interest in the history of Houston and led me to research the lives of its women.

Barbara Bolton of The Donning Company first suggested that this book be written, and it was through her encouragement that I undertook the project. My thanks go also to Nancy Geyer, Kathryn Schadewald, and Anne Sloan, who read the manuscript, and whose suggestions contributed to both clarity and relevance.

Assembling nearly three hundred photographs was a formidable task. Many individuals made suggestions, helped track down images, and in some cases provided images. These persons are too numerous to list. I am, however, deeply indebted to each of them. The staffs of various archival collections were extremely helpful as I sought appropriate photographs. One person especially went beyond the call of duty. Joel Draut, archival photographer with the Houston Metropolitan Research Center of the Houston Public Library, was of inestimable value in providing historical images.

My sincere gratitude for sharing their talents and time goes to Carole Halla for her intriguing dust jacket and to Jim Glass for his enlightening map of settlement in early Texas.

I thank the Houston Junior Forum for believing in this project enough to devote their time and energy to promote it. Jacque Royce and Saundra Adams have my deep appreciation for spearheading the Forum's efforts. Their enthusiasm has kept me at work all these months.

Most of all I am grateful to my husband, Bill, for his steadfast support, his computer expertise, and his sympathetic ear. I could not have done it without him.

This book is in no way a comprehensive survey of Houston women. It would take several volumes to tell the complete story. Obviously, many women worthy of mention have not been included in this narrative. This is only a beginning. I sincerely hope that future historians will relate more of the fascinating story of the women who have called Houston home.

Women have always worked, but their numbers in the workplace increased dramatically in the twentieth century as more job opportunities became available to them. They were employed in offices, stores, and factories. Eventually they entered professional fields as well. (Houston Metropolitan Research Center, Houston Public Library)

INTRODUCTION

A tapestry is made up of many individual threads. These are woven together to create a fabric, giving it strength, beauty, and—most importantly—wholeness. It takes all of the threads to produce the complete piece.

History is a tapestry. People, places, and events are the threads of time which reveal the past. Each is an essential part of the whole story. Recorded history, however, has not traditionally included all the threads. Women, one-half of the human race, have been virtually ignored by historians. Most readers would assume that women were merely bystanders totally uninvolved in the events of their time; yet, closer examination reveals that women have been an active and influential part of our history from the very founding of the nation. As scholars have delved into women's history over the last three decades, they have uncovered much about women's lives—their work, values, relationships, and achievements.

Texas did not provide a hospitable environment for its earliest residents. Life was difficult, even perilous, much of the time. Still women settled here with the same hopes and dreams as men. They were intent on building a future for themselves and their families. Whatever their ethnic background or economic status, their experiences were similar. They lived, married, bore children, wept, laughed, prayed, toiled, and died on the frontier, contributing greatly to the fabric of the new society.

When Houston was settled in the mid-nineteenth century, women were important as bearers of civilization to this untamed setting. While home and family remained at the core of their lives, women realized that their familial responsibilities led quite naturally into an expanded role as guardians of the entire community. Acceptance of this role helped women move from their private sphere into a more public one. As they encountered needs in the community, they threw themselves into new forms of activity. Through social work, agitation for reform, and political lobbying, women enlarged their sphere by becoming advocates for change and proponents for better living conditions. Over the years Houston's women have built viable community institutions that have become strong and lasting threads in the city's fabric. Education, the arts, welfare, health care—all have benefited through the efforts of visionary women who dared to make a difference.

A woman's sphere has also broadened to include the workplace. Although their presence in the labor force has until recently been unrecognized, women have always worked. Combating inadequate compensation and poor working conditions, women carved out their own niches, most frequently in domestic service, industry, and what came to be known as "pink collar jobs." Even when improvements in education enabled women to enter the professions in the early twentieth century, their positions in the workplace remained marginal. Still Houston's women have persisted in contributing their talents and skills toward developing a stronger and more prosperous city.

When we view our history as a multi-faceted tapestry, it is obvious that women of all stations in life have contributed threads to the fabric. While these women may have been historically invisible, they did play a significant role in the development of Houston.

This is their story.

Women cultivated the arts in Houston as performers, creators, and patrons. Having received her early instruction in Houston, Ernestine Jessie Covington graduated from Oberlin Conservatory and then attended New York's Julliard Musical Foundation. After completing her training in 1928, Covington spent several years on concert tours throughout the South. (Covington Collection, Houston Metropolitan Research Center, Houston Public Library)

As Houston's female community recognized needs in the city, they worked to meet those needs. Ruth Nicholson House served as the first president of Faith Home. Her leadership enabled the institution to build a strong foundation for the future. At the same time Mrs. House's responsibilities within her own family, with whom she is pictured here, reflected the dual roles many women assumed. (Ellen House Howze Papers, Junior League Component, Houston Metropolitan Research Center, Houston Public Library)

Working from a Texas Coastal Indian skull recovered in archaeological excavations on Galveston Island, forensic sculptor Betty Pat Gatliff reconstructed this woman's face, which was then cast in bronze. Such studies have provided valuable insights into the characteristics of aboriginal Texans. (Courtesy The Heritage Society; photo by author)

CHAPTER 1

Settling Texas

When the Spanish first explored the land which the natives called "Tejas" about 1528, the area in which Houston and Galveston are now situated was sparsely populated. The region was inhabited primarily by the Karankawan tribes. Since their presence was never recorded in a census and their names never appeared in a written narrative, the identities and accomplishments of individual Karankawas—especially the women—are unknown. It is generally accepted, however, that the first women indigenous to the area were Karankawas.

Like most Native Americans, the Karankawas followed a strictly defined gender-related division of labor. Men were the warriors, priests, and decision makers; women were the laborers. They were expected to bear and care for the young; prepare the dwelling; cook; tan the hides; and collect berries, herbs, and firewood. They not only produced many of the items used for tribal trade, but also most often made the cooking utensils, baskets, pottery, and household furnishings, even adorning these useful objects with their artistry. Álvar Núñez Cabeza de Vaca, the earliest of the Spanish explorers to interact with the natives, noted in his journal that "their women toil incessantly."

These women led a perilous existence. One common hazard was the unhealthy environment. Death rates for women of childbearing age were very high. Also hard work, frequent migrations, poor diet, and primitive medicines contributed to the heavy mortality among all Indian women.

The Texas Indian women were, however, at home in their surroundings. Their environment was a natural habitat—one in which they had fully developed institutions, well-established customs, and extended tribal and kinship groups. Unlike the women who would later migrate to this region, the Native American women had their civilization and culture intact.

This was not true of the Anglo women who ventured into Texas in the early nineteenth century. They had left familiar surroundings and loved ones to embark on an unfamiliar and uncertain life. Their journeys to this raw, largely unpopulated land were fraught with hardship.

From their home in New Jersey, newlywed Hannah Burnet traveled with her husband, David, aboard the *Call.* The vessel carried all of the couple's worldly goods, including materials for the sawmill they planned to build at their new home. As the boat entered Galveston Bay, a sudden storm grounded the ship on a sand bar near Bolivar Peninsula. The Burnets lost everything, and Hannah was forced to wade through the wild surf to begin her new life in Texas.

This replica of a Karankawan dwelling, based on contemporary accounts, was constructed utilizing materials indigenous to the Gulf Coast: willow, dwarf palmetto, cattail leaves, and oyster shells. In the Karankawas' migratory existence, this kind of hut was easily transported from place to place. (Courtesy Baytown Historical Museum; photo by author)

Indian women produced most of the utilitarian items used in their daily existence. Because the Karankawas were a migratory tribe, they probably carried few possessions with them as they moved. The fragments of this pot were excavated in the Baytown area and then reconstructed. (Courtesy Baytown Historical Museum; photo by author)

This braced-frame wood dwelling, located originally on the banks of Clear Creek, was typical of the homes in the Austin colony. Diaries and letters reveal how one occupant, Mary Duer, spent her days growing her family's food, nursing sick friends, and occasionally making the twenty-mile trip into Houston for supplies. (Photo by author)

Like Hannah Burnet, most pioneer women experienced great hardships as they came westward to this unknown frontier on foot or horseback, in oxen-drawn wagons, and on ocean vessels. Intent on establishing their households, tending their families, and surviving the wilderness, most came with husbands. Their lives as wives and mothers were not easy. But the tribulations faced by single women making this journey were even more burdensome.

Attracted by notices offering free fertile land in Texas, widow Sarah Smith sold her Arkansas farm, packed her household goods, and with her five children joined a wagon train bound for Texas in November 1833. The caravan was drenched by heavy rains; and when the group reached the Sabine River, it was in flood stage. Some of the travelers cut down wild mulberry trees and made a raft on which the families and their possessions were precariously transported across the swollen river. Once across, they still faced almost three hundred miles of trackless territory before they would reach their promised land in the Brazos River valley. Upon arrival, the energetic Sarah established her homestead, doing the heavy outside work herself.

Preparing meals was a laborious task for women. Most food was cooked in an open fireplace, although an outside fire was sometimes used to escape the stifling heat indoors. Diets were generally limited to foods that the family could raise itself. (Courtesy The Heritage Society)

In a back-breaking task, Hispanic women made meal from corn grown in gardens they tended. Every housewife possessed a *metate* on which the grain was ground before being made into tortillas and baked on a stone *comal*. (Drawing from "Woman Grinding on the Metate" by Frederic Remington, UT Institute of Texan Cultures at San Antonio)

In the absence of physicians on the frontier, women usually dispensed medicine to their families. A chest filled with homemade remedies was found in most homes. (Courtesy The Heritage Society)

Women were frequently subjected to moving. Catherine Sherman's life typified that of the wife of an entrepreneur on the Texas frontier. She lived first in a one-room cabin near San Jacinto and later moved from place to place as her husband pursued various enterprises. Trunks were a necessary item not only for transporting belongings but also for storing them. (Courtesy The Heritage Society)

Producing cloth was extremely time consuming for women. Two weeks of steady labor were required to spin enough thread for a dress. For those families fortunate enough to have a loom, it took an additional week to weave the fabric. These tasks were frequently performed by a female slave. (Texas State Library and Archives Commission)

Since the law required that a recipient of land be head of a house-hold, most land grants were conveyed to men. Some single women nevertheless received titles to land from *empresario* Stephen F. Austin. One grantee was Amy White. A widowed mother of ten, White was granted land along the San Jacinto River and moved there in 1824 with her four youngest children. Although she had relatives nearby, she managed her affairs herself. One year after settling on her land, she wrote to Austin as "a lone woman," seeking a resolution to a disputed survey of her property. Displaying the tenacity so typical of these pioneer women, Amy White was determined to protect her homestead and provide for her family.

Since Anglo settlements tended to be scattered, women often suffered a profound sense of isolation. As their husbands were frequently absent, these women were sometimes "quite overcome with lone," as one recorded in her diary. They had little opportunity to escape this solitude because there were few social organizations, no schools, and no churches. Many women felt not only utter loneliness but also terror in the isolation of their homes.

Jane Wilkins, a widow with two young daughters, journeyed from Alabama to settle in Texas. She erected a dwelling along Buffalo Bayou where the George R. Brown Convention Center is located today. Archaeological studies at the site uncovered artifacts which verified Mrs. Wilkins' presence there in 1822 and revealed aspects of everyday life in her household.
(Courtesy The Heritage Society; photo by author)

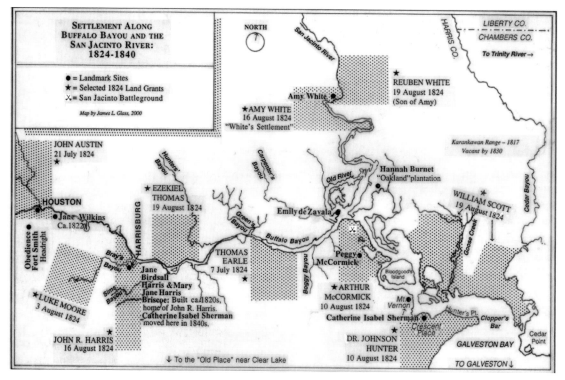

Women settled along Buffalo Bayou and the San Jacinto River during the colonial period and early years of the Republic. This map, drawn by James L. Glass, shows the location of their homesteads in proximity to one another. The drawing also indicates early land grants, the system under which Texas was first settled. (Map by James L. Glass, 2000)

Widowed Peggy McCormick ran a profitable cattle business on her land near the confluence of Buffalo Bayou and the San Jacinto River. Here in 1836 the Texan forces won independence from Mexico. Mrs. McCormick's land is now the site of the memorial to that confrontation. (Illustration by Jack Slattery, 1986)

In 1833 Mary Austin Holley wrote *Texas, Observations Historical, Geographical, and Descriptive*, the first book published in English in Texas. Her narrative encouraged prospective settlers to make Texas their home, but advised that everything useful must be brought with them. (Prints and Photographs Collection, Center for American History, University of Texas at Austin)

As a result of the absence of community, extended family, and church, these first generation Texans came to view themselves as civilizers and felt obligated to bring gentility, culture, and beauty to this raw life. The primitive nature of their existence inspired in women a creativity which was expressed in their quilts, basketry, flower gardens, and garments.

In the early years of settlement, a woman's role was chiefly within her own household. As husbands cleared the fields for pasture and crops, wives spun and wove cloth; raised and prepared food for the table; tried to keep the house clean; and made soap, candles, and medicine. Since farm goods were produced to be sold as well as consumed within the household, women were also important in the family's economic efforts.

Family health responsibilities added to the burdens of wives and mothers, who were the makers and dispensers of home remedies and chief caretakers of the sick. Frequent outbreaks of cholera and fevers, accidents, and childbirth took a frightful toll on pioneer women and their families. Pregnancies frequently ended in stillbirths, and children often died in infancy. Women were also expected to care for neighbors in times of sickness, death, or other crises. Hannah Burnet wrote her home remedies in a small leather notebook. Her cure for toothache "proceeding from whatever cause" was to apply a balsam made from "oil of origanum, oil of cloves, tincture of herbane, sweet spirits of nitric, tincture of opium and white wax." Her "infallible remedy for sore throat" was to "make a poultice of wormwood baked in sweet milk and apply to throat." Burnet, throughout her life, ministered to her neighbors.

While the presence of black women in the settlement of Texas can be documented, there are few accounts of their individual lives. Most were slaves, and

like Anglo women they also occupied the dual roles of familial caregiver and economic provider. A slave's labor, however, was done in support of her owner's well-being rather than that of her own family. Slave women in Texas were cooks, washerwomen, nurses, dairywomen, maids, midwives—roles considered appropriately domestic. In agricultural work women hoed, cleaned brush, stacked hay, and picked cotton. Many cotton plantations consistently numbered women among their top pickers.

Although servitude dictated a slave woman's very existence, no role was as important to her as that of wife and mother. Because slave marriages had no legal basis, few records were kept of such unions. Still, couples observed the creation of a family unit with some kind of ritual even it if was an informal ceremony. In spite of these attempts to solidify their roles as wives and mothers, slave women were frequently separated from their husbands and children through migration and sale. They knew little of security and stability.

On the frontier, the circumstances of mistress and slave were similar. Both faced loneliness, isolation, frequent male absence, wrenching displacement occasioned by migration to an unknown area, the absence of comforting institutions, and the precarious nature of medical care under generally unhealthy conditions. As a result, close reciprocal relationships often developed. While Jane Long kept a two-year vigil on Bolivar Peninsula awaiting her husband's return from Mexico, Kian, her young female slave, kept them alive during the bleak winter of 1820–21 by leaving the fortress at night to fish and seek oysters for Long and her hungry children. Throughout the rest of their lives, Jane Long and Kian experienced an unusually close relationship.

After her husband's death, Jane Long returned to Mississippi and later reentered Texas as part of Stephen F. Austin's colony. She operated an inn on her land grant near Richmond and later successfully managed her own plantation, which in 1850 was one of sixteen in Texas worth more than $10,000. This rendering of Mrs. Long and her slave, Kian, repulsing the Karankawas on Bolivar Peninsula was painted by Houston artist John Biggers. (UT Institute of Texan Cultures at San Antonio, courtesy Texas Southern University)

When the Republic of Texas banned free blacks, some petitioned the Texas Congress for the right to remain as citizens. Nurse Mary Madison's petition was granted after some white citizens attested to her capable and tender care of the sick. (Reprinted by permission of Ruth Winegarten, *Texas Women*, pg. 22)

The lives of free black women were just as precarious. They were few in number in Texas during the colonial period, and attempts were made to completely remove them in the early days of the Republic. Free blacks were required to petition the government for permission to remain. In 1837 Fannie McFarland, who had been emancipated by her owner, stated in her petition that she had put together a little property by her industry, prudence, and economy, and therefore wanted to stay in Texas. Although McFarland's petition was denied, she was allowed to remain. If free black women did stay, they were expected to justify their existence by providing useful service. A surprising number were self-supporting single heads of households—most of them cooks, laundresses, and seamstresses—whose talents were much in demand. A few free black women had their own farms, while Fannie McFarland engaged in real estate transactions and managed to make a profit on each one.

Hispanic women were in Texas before the colonial settlement by Stephen F. Austin. More than sixty Spanish and Mexican land grants were awarded directly to women. Others inherited land from their husbands or fathers. Some of these women controlled vast acreage and wealth. Doña María Hinijosa de Ballí was Texas' first cattle queen. She ultimately owned a third of the present lower Rio Grande Valley, including Padre Island, which was named after her son, a priest. María Cassiano was another influential woman. In 1808 she married the Spanish governor of Texas and ran the affairs of state in his absence. During this early period in Texas most Hispanic women, however, were not wealthy like Doña María Hinijosa de Ballí or influential like María Cassiano. Most worked hard as wives, mothers, farmers, shepherdesses, midwives, laundresses, cooks, peddlers, or potters. They were poor, and they remain almost entirely anonymous in history.

During the Texas Revolution women were called upon to help in the struggle for independence. Those of means often provided money and livestock for the cause, while others made cartridges and clothing for the army. When their menfolk left to join the Texas forces, women had to supervise farm work or do it themselves. As the Mexican armies drew further into Texas in early April of 1836, women—anxious for the safety of their families and themselves—evacuated eastward in what came to be known as the Runaway Scrape. Packing whatever belongings they could carry in wagons or on horseback, they fled toward the safety of the United States. Dilue Harris, then a young girl, later recorded her experience: "We left home at sunset, having clothes, bedding, and provisions on the sleigh with one yoke of oxen. Mother and I were walking, she with an infant in her arms. Brother drove the oxen, and my two little sisters rode in the sleigh." The hardships continued as Dilue and her family traveled congested roads and crossed the rising Trinity River. Dilue's little sister died, and her mother became seriously ill. The family, however, forged ahead until they received news of the Texas victory at San Jacinto.

Although the Runaway Scrape was a traumatic experience for Texas women, they coped well. Accustomed to hardship, they readily attended to one another. They cared for each other's children, shared food and shelter, and helped bury the dead. White and black women experienced similar living conditions. Then, when peace came to the Texas Republic, women resumed their lives much as before.

During the early years of settlement, Texas women, regardless of status, were effective workers, becoming more independent and exercising authority, especially within the family. They did so, however, within the traditional framework of their societies. Women contributed substantially to Texas during its frontier period, but their great resources were used in supportive roles. The journey from a separate and limited sphere to a larger one still lay ahead.

Women supported the struggle for Texas independence in a variety of ways. Sarah Dodson of Harrisburg stitched this flag from squares of fabric for her husband's militia unit to carry into battle in 1835. It is often considered Texas's first "Lone Star" flag. (Courtesy Glendale Cemetery Association, Houston)

Emily West de Zavala, whose husband was the first vice president of the Republic of Texas, was forced in April 1836 to flee her home on Buffalo Bayou in the wake of the approaching Mexican army. Following the battle at San Jacinto, the Zavala home was used as a hospital. Emily survived three husbands, remaining in the area until her death in 1882. (UT Institute of Texan Cultures at San Antonio, courtesy University of Incarnate Word, San Antonio)

Jane Birdsall Harris lost her home when Harrisburg, a town founded by her late husband, was burned just prior to the Battle of San Jacinto. This replacement, on a site overlooking Buffalo Bayou, was sometimes used by Mrs. Harris as an inn. (Knox Briscoe Howe Papers, Junior League Component, Houston Metropolitan Research Center, Houston Public Library)

Above: Obedience Fort Smith, a sixty-four-year-old widow, immigrated to Texas in 1835. She was granted 3,370 acres of land, which encompassed much of present-day Houston's Fourth Ward, Montrose, and Rice University neighborhoods. The area is still named on legal documents as the Obedience Smith Survey. (The Heritage Society)

Above right: In 1852 Jane Choate Owens paid $1,000 for property on Clear Creek. There she and her husband reared a family of eight children and used the land for running cattle. Mrs. Owens engaged in another common enterprise at the time—taking boarders into her home. (The Heritage Society)

Bottom right: Women in rural Texas filled many roles—wife, mother, neighbor, farm worker, nurse, teacher, seamstress, and house-keeper. Families were often large, and long hours of toil were required to meet their needs. (Houston Metropolitan Research Center, Houston Public Library)

The Second Great Awakening of the early nineteenth century brought large numbers of women into formal church membership. Pious females were encouraged to become active participants, especially in Protestant churches. In Houston women were involved as founders and congregants of the local Methodist, Baptist, and Presbyterian churches shown here in this 1852 painting. (Courtesy Jean B. Salvado)

CHAPTER II

Defining Woman's Sphere

On January 2, 1839, the *Rufus Putnam* landed at the foot of Houston's Main Street after making a hazardous journey up Buffalo Bayou. Among its passengers was Millie Gray, who with her six children had come to Houston to join her husband in establishing their new home. The small, primitive town which awaited Mrs. Gray was a far cry from the settled, civilized Virginia she had left. In her diary she recorded her thoughts after stepping ashore that day: "Although everything looks better than I had expected, my heart feels oppressed & it requires an effort to wear the appearance of cheerfulness. I could (if I were a weeping character) sit down and fairly weep . . ." Millie Gray, however, was not a weeping character. She, along with other women who settled here, became a mainstay of the young community.

The rigors of settling Texas had permitted little distinction between men's and women's tasks and responsibilities, but as Houston became a thriving commercial town, a woman's role was redefined. Now her place was a well-defined sphere of influence which focused on the home and the family. The ideology of "True Womanhood," which permeated society, emphasized four cardinal virtues—piety, purity, submission, and domesticity. Although the idealization of these attributes was actually relevant only to the married middle-class woman, the standards that it set affected many other females as well. This female sphere limited women's economic options to providing domestic goods and services, but it did enlarge women's social responsibilities, encouraging them to make the community a more virtuous place.

A woman's sphere outside the home was defined to a large degree by her religious activities. The popular literature of the period described women as especially pious, having a unique responsibility to maintain and spread their faith. In Houston, as in most of the nation, women participated in the formation of the first churches and constituted the majority of their members. Like their counterparts in the United States, they organized women's societies that enabled them to promote their own projects and to control them.

In 1841 Baptists in Houston organized a church with twenty-three charter members, sixteen of them female. Two of these women, Piety Hadley and Charlotte Fuller, were given the responsibility of raising money to erect the first church building. Accepting a skinny mule as a donation, they fattened up their acquisition and then sold it. Their project was underway. Thirty years later the Baptist ladies were told once again to raise funds for a larger building. They held cake sales, box suppers, auctions, and craft bazaars to provide for a new church.

There were no female charter members of Houston's first Episcopal congregation. Women nevertheless played a significant role in church affairs, participating unofficially through their own organization. Apparently organized as early as 1850, the Sewing Circle of Christ Church did much more than sew. In 1851 the group asked the vestry to lease an old schoolhouse. The women agreed to pay the rent, repair the building, and manage its use while giving all the income to the parish. Their real objective was to have facilities for the Sunday School. They later raised funds to make improvements to their church building, purchase prayer books, contribute to the minister's salary, and establish a home for "old, indigent ladies."

The Ladies' Association of the Presbyterian congregation entered upon its church-wide efforts with some apprehension. Their president reported, "Timid, fearing lest inexperienced feet might lead us into some debtors' slough of despond, we took our first steps forward." Little did the Presbyterian women realize that over the next three decades they would undertake the entire cost of the church's first manse, lend the church an immense sum on a later church edifice, and build an entire hospital wing.

Realizing that their own organizations allowed them to increase their roles within the church and at the same time encouraged the development

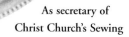

As secretary of Christ Church's Sewing Circle, Millie Gray penned the petitions in which the ladies made their not-so-gentle requests of the church vestry. Mrs. Gray's diary reveals much about life in early Houston from the perspective of one who was a wife, mother, neighbor, churchwoman, and citizen. (Courtesy Christ Church Cathedral)

of a female community, Houston women formed a group within each church. They had a variety of names: Piety Hadley Sewing Circle, which later became the Woman's Missionary Union; Ladies' Parish Association, descended from the Christ Church Sewing Circle; Ladies' Association of First Presbyterian Church; Methodist Ladies' Aid; Ladies' Hebrew Benevolent Association of Congregation Beth Israel; and, after the Civil War, Antioch Baptist Missionary Society. Their work, however, did not give them any real authority in the affairs of their congregations. Many church bodies agreed with the General Assembly of the Presbyterian Church when it cautioned, "It is not proper for girls and young women to preside over a meeting of a mixed society or to make addresses or to lead in prayer."

While women received no official recognition for assuming the seemingly unpleasant tasks of raising money and meeting physical needs of their congregations, they were in reality forging new trails by taking the initiative and assuming responsibilities outside their usual domain—the home. At the same time, they were recognizing larger needs in the community.

From 1861 to 1865 the energies of Houston women were diverted from church activities to the Civil War. This conflict, which shook American society to its foundations, had a marked influence on the lives of women. From its beginning women congregated in homes and churches to roll bandages, sew clothing, and organize fund-raising events. They also nursed the wounded and dying. During these years women gained a variety of new skills. They learned to speak in public and to handle finances. Many moved into formerly male jobs. In the absence of husbands and fathers they became the arbiters, decision makers, and disciplinarians in their families.

The Civil War radically changed the lives of black women by giving

Jane Avery came to Houston in 1842 as a young woman of twenty-two. After marrying Peter Gray, she became a dedicated member of Christ Church. In 1871 she was a cofounder of the Ladies' Parish Association, later serving as its president for eleven years. (Christ Church Collection, Houston Metropolitan Research Center, Houston Public Library)

In 1893 the Sheltering Arms Association was organized with seven members of the Ladies' Parish Association of Christ Church as charter members. Recognizing a need within their congregation, they opened this home for elderly women. Sheltering Arms Senior Services still provides support for Houston's older population. (Courtesy Sheltering Arms Senior Services)

Sophronia Cone joined Houston's Presbyterian church on December 25, 1839, and immediately became an untiring participant in congregational activities—teaching, ministering to those in need, providing music for worship services, and serving as a Home Missionary. (Courtesy First Presbyterian Church)

Mary Jane Harris Briscoe, member of a pioneer Texas family, was herself a pioneer in the development of Houston. She served as the first president of Sheltering Arms' home for aged women. Meetings in her home gave birth to both the Ladies' Reading Club and the Daughters of the Republic of Texas. The continued existence of these organizations testifies to Mrs. Briscoe's vision. (Houston Metropolitan Research Center, Houston Public Library)

To underwrite their activities, the Presbyterian Ladies' Association compiled *The Texas Cookbook, A Thorough Treatise on the Art of Cookery* in 1883. The first cookbook published in the state, it included not only "receipts" but also "helpful household hints" appropriate in Houston's climate. (Houston Metropolitan Research Center, Houston Public Library)

Women formed the nucleus of church workers in the nineteenth century, as seen at a gathering of Christ Church's Sunday School teachers in the 1880s. (Houston Metropolitan Research Center, Houston Public Library)

MISCELLANEOUS RECEIPTS.

Measures for Housekeepers.

One quart wheat flour makes one pound.
One quart soft butter makes one pound.
One quart broken loaf sugar makes one pound.
One quart best brown sugar makes one pound, two ounces.
One quart white sugar powdered, makes one pound, one ounce.
Ten eggs make one pound.
Sixteen large tablespoonfuls make one-half pint.
Eight large tablespoonfuls make one gill.
Common sized tumbler holds one-half pint.
Sixty drops make one teaspoonful.

To Prevent Mildew on Preserves.

Take the white of an egg, and wet slightly both sides of a piece of paper large enough to cover the top of the preserves. It will keep them free from mold or spoiling for two years.

Another way is to wet in alcohol papers size of jars and lay over top of preserves.

Japanese Cleaning Cream.

One ounce castile soap, one ounce ammonia, one-half ounce glycerine, one-half ounce spirits of wine, one-half ounce ether. Put all in a quart bottle and fill with rainwater.

It will not spot the most delicate colors. Is excellent to remove spots from black goods.

Mrs. H. L. Carmer.

Cologne Water.

To one quart of alcohol add sixty drops of lavender, sixty drops of bergamot, sixty drops of essence of lemon, sixty drops of orange water, sixty drops of attar of roses.

Mrs. A. L. Lacey.

Mrs. S. G. Kay served in many capacities in the Methodist Episcopal Church: Sunday School Superintendent, choir director, and even as chairman of the Board of Stewards. A public school teacher and principal, Mrs. Kay was also involved in community activities, especially the YWCA. (Houston Metropolitan Research Center, Houston Public Library)

Jeannette Kimball Ennis became involved in church and club activities befitting the wife of a prominent Houston businessman. Mrs. Ennis's status is evidenced by her fashionable clothing, possibly purchased during a lengthy visit to Paris in the 1860s while her six daughters studied there. (Houston Metropolitan Research Center, Houston Public Library)

Charlotte Baldwin Allen, wife of Houston founder Augustus C. Allen, likely used some of her inheritance to provide money needed by her husband and his brother to purchase the site for Houston. Mrs. Allen was active in civic, religious, and business activities until her death in 1895. (Houston Metropolitan Research Center, Houston Public Library)

As the wife of the wealthiest man in the community, Margaret Bremond Rice occupied a special place in Houston society. During the Civil War, she worked tirelessly to raise money and to furnish supplies for the Confederacy. Her death in 1863 at the age of thirty may have been caused by nursing sick and wounded soldiers. (Woodson Research Center, Fondren Library, Rice University)

them freedom and by legalizing their marriages. This resulted in a widespread move to formalize individual marriages and to establish stable families in which both parents were recognized. Former slaves worked diligently to locate spouses or children who had been sold away from them. Although marriage and the family were now recognized legally, most blacks remained financially insecure. A large number of newly-freed black women labored in the fields or factories to supplement the meager incomes of their families. Houston's growth created a huge demand for domestic servants and laundry workers, the occupations most available to urban black women.

After the war, black neighborhoods or "freedmen's towns" sprang up. Newly emancipated women put tremendous effort into their communities by organizing churches, schools, and public and private events. Churches became the social bases of operation for black women, just as they had been for white ones. Black women supported their churches by giving and raising funds, forming missionary societies, and even becoming missionaries themselves.

On Christmas Eve 1862 the ladies of Houston and Harrisburg organized a benefit which raised $250 for the local hospital for Confederate troops. For another such function, they gathered sewing machines, musical instruments, fancy clothing, and gold jewelry to be sold at auction. (Special Collections, Houston Public Library)

Popular publications of the period, such as *Godey's Lady's Book*, though stressing that women were the moral guardians of society, also advocated the expansion of the female sphere through improved education and the employment of women as teachers. Opponents of female education, however, propagated the belief that mental activity would weaken the female constitution and interfere with a woman's desire and ability to bear children. Physical anthropologists contributed to the argument against educating women with the discovery that females had smaller brains than males. They concluded, and explicitly pronounced, that there was a direct correlation between intelligence and brain size. Science has since established that their conclusions were totally erroneous.

In spite of such opposition, educational facilities for females were expanded. By 1845 the Houston Academy was in existence, and although they were instructed in separate rooms, girls were offered the same curriculum as boys. They first took reading, writing, and orthography; then proceeded to arithmetic, grammar, and geography; and concluded with courses in Latin, Greek, philosophy, and "higher matter." This was more extensive schooling than females received in many other towns in the region. At the same time, however, the all-male Houston Lyceum was

In 1851 Zerviah Noble advertised the opening of a school for "Misses, generally, and Masters under the ages of twelve." The private school in her home later became a part of Houston's public school system. Mrs. Noble's granddaughter, Eloise Szabo (shown in the photograph with her), was one of the first female principals in the city. (The Heritage Society)

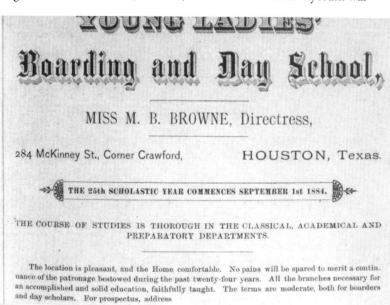

YOUNG LADIES'

Boarding and Day School,

MISS M. B. BROWNE, Directress,

284 McKinney St., Corner Crawford,   HOUSTON, Texas.

THE 25th SCHOLASTIC YEAR COMMENCES SEPTEMBER 1st 1884.

THE COURSE OF STUDIES IS THOROUGH IN THE CLASSICAL, ACADEMICAL AND PREPARATORY DEPARTMENTS.

The location is pleasant, and the Home comfortable. No pains will be spared to merit a continuance of the patronage bestowed during the past twenty-four years. All the branches necessary for an accomplished and solid education, faithfully taught. The terms are moderate, both for boarders and day scholars. For prospectus, address

Miss Browne's Young Ladies' Seminary opened in 1859. Its founder, Mary B. Browne, taught not only embroidery, music, and dancing—long considered suitable accomplishments for females—but she also emphasized basic academic courses. This school, referred to as the "Vassar of the South" by the *Houston Post* in 1886, existed until the 1890s. (*1885 Directory for the City of Houston*, Houston Public Library)

Although largely self-taught as a botanist, Maude Fuller Young conducted extensive research while teaching in a local school. In 1873 she wrote *Familiar Lessons in Botany with a Flora of Texas, Adapted to General Use in the Southern States*, thought to be the first scientific textbook published in Texas. (Houston Metropolitan Research Center, Houston Public Library)

debating the question, "Are women capable of the same mental improvement as men?"

Since caring for children was considered an inherent skill of women, and since a female teacher required little more than a grade-school education herself, teaching became an increasingly attractive occupation for women. Houston's earliest schools were small and were conducted as private enterprises in homes or churches, most frequently by females in the community.

Teaching was the only profession open to black women. They began teaching in Freedmen's Bureau schools soon after the Civil War. When public education began in the 1870s, they taught in segregated public schools. Like their white counterparts, they too had limited opportunities for their own education. The Houston school system did not have a high school until 1878; one was not available for the city's black youth until 1892. In the last decade of the nineteenth century, however, educational opportunities increased for both white and black women who wanted to teach. New normal schools and teacher training institutions opened in Texas. By 1900 the teaching profession was largely feminized. In spite of these gains, female teachers were almost invariably paid less than males, and administrative positions were usually reserved exclusively for men.

Sisters from the Congregation of the Incarnate Word and Blessed Sacrament traveled from France to Houston in 1873 to start a school for girls. They opened Incarnate Word Academy, which has been educating females at the same site for more than 125 years. The building shown here has been in use since 1905. (Photo by author)

In the mid-1880s the American Baptist Women's Home Mission Society of Chicago sent Jennie Peck and Florence Dysart to Houston. Working with the Reverend Jack Yates, they established Houston Academy. (Jack Yates Collection, Houston Metropolitan Research Center, Houston Public Library)

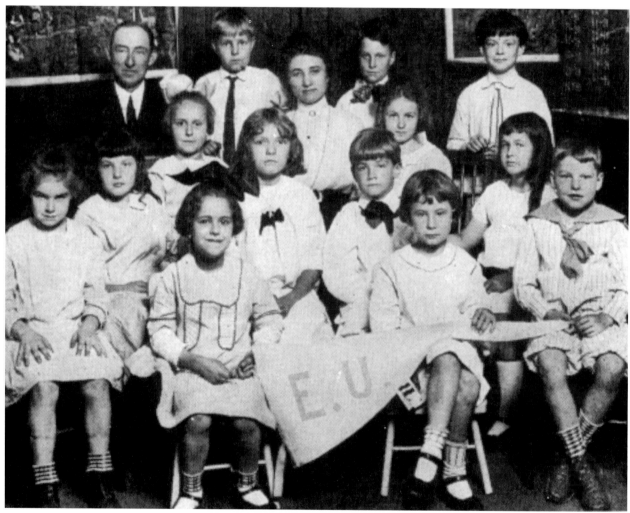

Schools were frequently housed in churches. In 1907 Jennie Eichler received permission to open a school in Christ Church's parish house. She soon had three primary classes in operation, one of which is pictured with her. (Cora Conner Spear Papers, Junior League Component, Houston Metropolitan Research Center, Houston Public Library)

Pinky Yates, encouraged by her father who greatly valued education, was afforded the unusual opportunity in the late 1890s of attending Spelman Female Seminary in Atlanta for her high school education. After taking the course designed for teacher education, she returned to Houston and began teaching in the public schools. (Jack Yates Collection, Houston Metropolitan Research Center, Houston Public Library)

After teaching in the public schools, Pearl Lights organized a kindergarten at Antioch Baptist Church in 1910. She envisioned not only a modern kindergarten but also a day nursery for working mothers. Her dream was finally realized after her death. (Houston Metropolitan Research Center, Houston Public Library)

The 1910 graduating class of Houston High School poses on the front steps of the school. During the early years of secondary education, females could choose among three courses of study: classical, general, or normal. (Houston Metropolitan Research Center, Houston Public Library)

To compensate for their lack of formal education, local women began organizing clubs in which they could discuss intellectual matters in acceptable surroundings. By the 1880s, middle-class women were forming clubs at a rapid pace. These clubs offered women exposure to new ideas and new friendships and above all enabled them to develop respect for their own talents and potentialities. As members gained self-confidence and organizational skills, they looked beyond their own intellectual improvement and sought ways to improve their communities. As a result, women's organizations became catalysts for social change as well as informal centers of information and ideologies.

Through their clubs and church soci-

The Ladies' Reading Club, organized in 1885, was Houston's first women's club. The group concentrated on art, literature, history, and science, with members presenting carefully researched papers. The club still exists 115 years later. (Ladies' Reading Club Collection, Houston Metropolitan Research Center, Houston Public Library)

In 1893 eight female parishioners at Annunciation Catholic Church met to form the Woman's Club. Belle Sherman Kendall, an early president, was one of the members who solicited the help of Andrew Carnegie in building a public library. The Woman's Club is still active today. (Houston Metropolitan Research Center, Houston Public Library)

In 1902 fourteen young women organized the Married Ladies Social, Art and Charity Club. Its purpose as stated in the bylaws was to inspire its members through intellectual, artistic, and civic pursuits, and to engage in benevolent undertakings in the city. **The group is still in existence today.** (The Married Ladies Social, Art and Charity Club Collection, Houston Metropolitan Research Center, Houston Public Library)

Since most women's clubs were constantly in search of a meeting place, the Houston Heights Woman's Club erected its own building. The lot on Harvard Street was donated by Mrs. D. D. Cooley, and the entire cost of its construction was paid off one year after its completion in 1912. The building is listed in the National Register of Historic Places. (Photo by author)

eties, women came to the realization that when they combined their efforts in a common purpose, they gained strength. When Kezia de Pelchin died in 1893, it appeared that her vision of a home for deprived children might die with her. Club women and members of female church organizations immediately came together to ensure that Mrs. de Pelchin's dream would become a reality. They had no guidelines to follow in establishing an institution of this magnitude. Undeterred, however, they obtained a charter, selected an all-female board, raised funds to operate the facility, and solicited the help of the entire community in providing services. They then began a hands-on operation in which Faith Home, as they named it, took root as a place dedicated to meeting the needs of children.

The last quarter of the nineteenth century was a time of important transition for women. The challenges of the war years had prepared Houston's women to meet the challenges of a growing city. New technology reduced the time required to maintain their households and created more leisure for many women. Desire for a better quality of life in the community led them to work collectively for improvements. Houston's women began slowly moving from their parlors into the public arena, where their presence would make a profound difference.

Kezia de Pelchin spent her life in service to others. As she nursed yellow fever victims and taught the young, she displayed deep compassion for those in distress. Her last humanitarian effort was in providing a home for children in need of a stable environment. Her legacy continues today through DePelchin Children's Center. (Houston Metropolitan Research Center, Houston Public Library)

Women's involvement at Faith Home is reflected in this cornerstone from its first building in 1897. Carved into the stone are the names of Mrs. Charles House as Chairman of the Building Committee and Mrs. M. E. Bryan as the Auditor. (Photo by author)

Married at the age of nineteen, Harriet Alice Owens experienced life as a typical wife and mother in the 1880s. (The Heritage Society)

Enedelia Rivera and Augustin Villagomez were married in 1921 at Our Lady of Guadalupe Church. Family and church were important aspects of Mexican-American women's lives in the 1920s. (Villagomez Family Collection, Houston Metropolitan Research Center, Houston Public Library)

Constance Houston and Tracy Thompson were married in 1928. During the next fifty years the Thompson's home, known as "Houston Place," was the setting for hundreds of weddings, receptions, and other social events for residents of their Fifth Ward neighborhood, whom they considered their extended family. (Joshua Houston Collection, Houston Metropolitan Research Center, Houston Public Library)

Motherhood was at the heart of many women's lives. Mrs. M. L. Westheimer, shown here with her family in 1912, was mother to sixteen children: eight of her own, five of relatives, and three orphans. (Jacolyn Alexander Papers, Junior League Component, Houston Metropolitan Research Center, Houston Public Library)

It was not unusual in the early twentieth century for an extended family to live together. Odelia and Henry Staiti's residence on Westmoreland was frequently home to a number of their sisters and brothers, seen here at a Sunday afternoon gathering. (The Heritage Society)

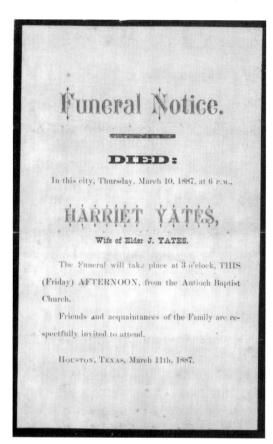

Funeral Notice.

DIED:

In this city, Thursday, March 10, 1887, at 6 P.M.,

HARRIET YATES,

Wife of Elder J. YATES.

The Funeral will take place at 3 o'clock, THIS (Friday) AFTERNOON, from the Antioch Baptist Church.

Friends and acquaintances of the Family are respectfully invited to attend.

HOUSTON, TEXAS, March 11th, 1887.

In the nineteenth century, about the only time a woman's name would appear in print was when she died. Harriet Yates, a former slave, lived in the Fourth Ward where she reared nine children and served as a pastor's wife. Her life was that of devoted wife, mother, and churchwoman. (Jack Yates Collection, Houston Metropolitan Research Center, Houston Public Library)

Women's lives changed dramatically as they encountered new inventions such as the automobile. Many, like Jenny Bering, became enthusiastic advocates for this conveyance that gave them increased independence and mobility. (Vernon Frost Papers, Junior League Component, Houston Metropolitan Research Center, Houston Public Library)

Women continued to play an important role in their church congregations, especially in times of change. This group, known informally as "Mothers of the Church," is shown in front of the new building being erected for Pleasant Grove Missionary Baptist Church in 1947. (Pleasant Grove Missionary Baptist Church Collection, Houston Metropolitan Research Center, Houston Public Library)

A large group attended the annual meeting of the Women's Missionary Society at El Mesias Methodist Church in 1938. Church activities were a significant part of women's lives in this north side neighborhood. (Rachel Lucas Collection, Houston Metropolitan Research Center, Houston Public Library)

In 1925 the Sisterhood of Congregation Adath Yeshurun was formed. It was active in all of the congregation's affairs, especially those pertaining to education. Shown in this photograph, circa 1927, is the Religious School's faculty comprised partly of female members of the congregation. (Houston Metropolitan Research Center, Houston Public Library)

Houston's first public library was established through the determined efforts of the city's club women. Upon its completion, two women—Belle Kendall and Elizabeth Ring—were named to the library's Board of Trustees. Today there are ten branch libraries named for local women. (Houston Metropolitan Research Center, Houston Public Library)

CHAPTER III

Building Community Institutions

The mayor and city aldermen gathered in the quarters of the Houston Lyceum on the afternoon of January 23, 1899, at the invitation of the Ladies' Reading Club. After providing musical entertainment and refreshments—chicken salad, hot biscuits, and coffee—the women pointed to the empty bookshelves and reminded the city fathers that they had failed in their promise to provide an adequate library for the town's residents. Apparently caught off-guard by the women's tenacity and boldness, the mayor immediately agreed to recommend a $200 monthly assessment for a public facility. The club secretary concluded her minutes that day with, "Hope, like the gleaming light, adorns and cheers our way." After Houston's women's clubs combined their efforts to secure funds to purchase a library site, they successfully solicited money from industrialist Andrew Carnegie for a building. On March 2, 1904, the Houston Lyceum and Carnegie Library was dedicated. Clearly, the city's females were assuming new roles in the community.

Women's grand entrance into the public arena occurred in the summer of 1893 at the Women's Congress, a significant and highly visible part of the World's Columbian Exposition at Chicago. The Exposition attracted over twenty-seven million visitors to the city. The event not only signaled that the United States was to become a world power; it also reminded the world of the contributions that women were making through their organizational talents and volunteerism. Texas women, who with their sisters from across the nation had participated in the event, returned to their homes with added fervor to make a difference in their communities.

At the beginning of the twentieth century, most middle-class women still believed in the paramount importance of their role as mothers and homemakers. Yet life in the home was changing for many women. Houstonians could now buy a wide variety of edible products and clothing: baked goods, canned vegetables, suits, shirts, and dresses. Many homes had hot and cold indoor running water. Heat was provided by furnaces run on oil, coal, or gas. Stoves were fueled by gas. Delivery services provided ice for refrigerators. Electric power was available in many parts of the city for lamps, sewing machines, irons, and vacuum cleaners. By the early 1900s the first electric washing machines were on the market. These technological developments, along with the reality of smaller families, created more leisure time for middle-class women. As a result, women extended their domestic skills to the community at large, becoming "municipal housekeepers."

Houston's population had mushroomed from 9,832 in 1870 to 44,633 by 1900. Local government found itself stymied by the social and economic problems created by this rapid growth. City leaders had difficulty providing clean water and collecting growing piles of garbage, and they were virtually helpless in matters of public health, education, and cultural enrichment. Cognizant of these problems, women set about collectively to find solutions.

The City Federation of Women's Clubs was organized in 1900 to spur the formation of a public library. Adele Briscoe Looscan, the first president, maintained a strong interest in Houston's library throughout her life. She was herself an author, contributing many historical writings to Texas archival collections. (Houston Metropolitan Research Center, Houston Public Library)

Mae Harper Baines, shown with a photograph of Woman's Christian Temperance Union founder Frances Willard, was a leader in the work of local temperance units. Like many WCTU members, Mrs. Baines also worked for community improvements including the first underpass in the city. (University of Texas Institute of Texan Cultures at San Antonio, *San Antonio Light* Collection)

Their first efforts at correcting what they perceived to be community ills was directed toward banning the sale of whiskey. They viewed drinking as a primary cause of spouse and child abuse and believed prohibition could save the family, reduce crime, and alleviate poverty. The Woman's Christian Temperance Union, which led the struggle against liquor, soon expanded its crusade to combat other social ills, including unsafe work conditions, inadequate schools, and urban decay. Participation in the WCTU

Although Carry Nation, remembered for her famous hatchet, lived in Texas in the 1880s and ran a hotel in Richmond, it was after she left the state that she became an extremist in the prohibition movement. She is pictured here on a crusading visit to Houston in 1902. (Houston Metropolitan Research Center, Houston Public Library)

Carrying their homemade candle holders, members of a Mothers' Club prepared to go Christmas caroling. The first Mother's Club in the city was organized at Charlotte B. Allen School, the first in Houston named for a woman. (Courtesy Bernice Hale)

gave its members the courage and experience to speak in public, collect petitions, and write newspaper articles. While Houston's WCTU units were never as strong as those elsewhere in Texas, their rallying cry—

"agitate, educate, organize"—was adopted by many women who shared their desire to improve the quality of life in the city.

As mothers, women had an intrinsic interest in child welfare. Always mindful of the importance of education in a child's development, women organized Mothers' Clubs in the public schools. They worked to provide hot lunches, sanitary drinking fountains, playground equipment, musical instruments, and better physical facilities. The Texas Congress of Mothers, which later became the Parent Teachers Association, was organized in 1909 to lobby for legislation to benefit children. By 1918 there were Mothers' Clubs in thirty-six local schools. PTA organizations today continue their tradition of service to school children.

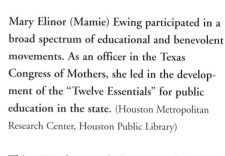

Mary Elinor (Mamie) Ewing participated in a broad spectrum of educational and benevolent movements. As an officer in the Texas Congress of Mothers, she led in the development of the "Twelve Essentials" for public education in the state. (Houston Metropolitan Research Center, Houston Public Library)

This 1903 photograph shows one of Houston's first kindergartens, which were organized by women and first conducted in private facilities. Women were persistent in lobbying for public kindergartens, which were finally approved by the Texas legislature in 1917. (Houston Metropolitan Research Center, Houston Public Library)

The Kindergarten Association at Antioch Baptist Church grew from the Daily Bible Classes instituted in 1910 by Pearl Lights. By 1915 a modern kindergarten and day care program were being conducted at the church by qualified teachers. (Houston Metropolitan Research Center, Houston Public Library)

As a public school teacher and a member of the Woman's Club, Mary Edna (Mamie) Gearing was instrumental in starting the first kindergarten class in the city. Miss Gearing later established the School of Domestic Economy at the University of Texas, eventually becoming the first woman to serve as full professor and department chair. (Prints and Photographs Collection, Center for American History, University of Texas at Austin)

Mothers' Clubs instituted domestic science classes in public schools by assuming financial responsibility for them. These women believed that courses in domestic science—later called home economics—as well as manual training for boys, were an important addition to students' learning and potential earning ability. (Houston Metropolitan Research Center, Houston Public Library)

Mothers were enthusiastic supporters of school projects through such organizations as the Parent-Teachers Association, shown here at Briscoe School in 1940. (Houston Metropolitan Research Center, Houston Public Library)

Although at the turn of the century art had almost no part in the lives of the city's residents, another group of women firmly believed that art education should be part of every child's learning experience. In 1900 the Public School Art League was organized for the purpose of placing reproductions of famous artwork in public schools. This coalition of club women and school teachers began purchasing pieces of art and distributing them to the schools, along with a course of study. During the next ten years it placed artwork in the schools at a cost of $22,000, a sizable sum in those days. The organization then expanded its agenda to include the city's adult population and began to acquire original art for a permanent collection. In 1912 the Public School Art League was renamed the Houston Art League and began planning a museum to house its growing collections. Its mission was completed in 1924 when the Museum of Fine Arts opened as the first municipal art museum in Texas. From its modest beginnings, this institution—created largely through the efforts of visionary Houston women—has grown into one of the nation's preeminent art museums.

Artist Emma Richardson Cherry provided strong leadership in the organization of the Public School Art League. She continued her involvement with the Museum of Fine Arts as an exhibitor and educator for the next forty years. (The Heritage Society)

This plaster image of Venus de Milo was purchased by the Public School Art League as part of their art education program. When the all-male school board rejected the piece as inappropriate for a school, the ladies presented it to the Houston Public Library where it has resided for ninety-six years. (Photo by author)

The Houston Art League was led by Florence Fall during eight years of raising funds and acquiring artwork for the city's first art museum. Art was not Mrs. Fall's only interest, however. As president of the Texas Federation of Women's Clubs in 1915, she was instrumental in the passage of the state's statute requiring compulsory school attendance. (Houston Metropolitan Research Center, Houston Public Library)

When Houston's Museum of Fine Arts opened on April 12, 1924, Houston's women were justifiably proud of their accomplishment in planting the seeds of art education in the city. However, in what became common procedure, men were appointed to fill board positions and to manage the museum's affairs. (Houston Metropolitan Research Center, Houston Public Library)

In an unprecedented action, a delegation of women visited City Hall in 1899 and made an appeal to the mayor for park land. As a result, acreage was purchased for the city's first public park. City Park—later renamed Sam Houston Park—became popular with Houstonians of all ages. (Postcard from author's collection)

Julia Hadley Franklin served as the first president of the Civic Club, guiding it in making Houston a cleaner, safer, and more beautiful place in which to live. (Houston Metropolitan Research Center, Houston Public Library)

Acutely aware of the detrimental effects of industrialization and urbanization upon their environment, Houston's women did not limit their activism to education and the arts. In 1901 club woman Margaret Hadley Foster issued a plea to the women of Houston. In a lengthy newspaper appeal she pointed out exigent conditions in the city: the polluted bayou, decrepit buildings, treacherous sidewalks, poor sanitation, and the lack of public recreational areas. Foster called for women to organize "not for pleasure, but for earnest, faithful work." The resulting Civic Club set about doing just that by organizing an adjunct club in each of the city's six wards. These groups successfully secured park land, provided playground equipment, and sponsored free park concerts. In the area of sanitation, they lobbied for city ordinances requiring covers on garbage cans and forbidding spitting on city streets, a practice which women viewed as a menace to public health. They also pushed for the Pure Food and Milk Law which was passed by the state legislature in 1907. To enhance the beauty of the city, they planted trees and flowers on school grounds and other public spaces. Insisting that they were not "meddling in politics," the Civic Club forced action which improved the quality of life for Houston's residents. It also set the pattern for the multitude of neighborhood civic clubs which exist in the city today.

While the concerns of the Civic Club were directed toward all sections of the city, some neighborhoods had greater needs than others. This was particularly true of the city's Second Ward, where by 1905 large numbers of immigrants had settled. An awareness of the crowded, impoverished conditions in this area led a group of women to form the Houston Settlement Association. Patterned after settlement houses in New York and Chicago, these women instituted sweeping programs to extend educational, industrial, social, and friendly aid to all those within their reach. Their focus on education included conducting a kindergarten, teaching adult English classes, establishing a circulating library, and holding cooking and sewing classes which ultimately evolved into domestic science

classes in the public schools. To combat unhealthy conditions within the neighborhood, the Settlement Association opened a dispensary, established the city's first well-baby clinic, and organized a staff of visiting nurses who provided home care for neighborhood residents. Although the Settlement Association was successful in improving the quality of life for Second Ward residents, its members realized that solutions depending on individual acts of mercy were not the best approach. As a result, they continually worked for the organization of permanent agencies to address the welfare of the entire community.

Houston's progressive-minded women soon realized that legislation was the key to ensuring permanent improvements within the community. Through the networking of the City Federation of Women's Clubs and its allied group, the Texas Federation of Women's Clubs, they kept issues before the appropriate bodies. Between 1909 and 1917, women's groups across the state came together to form powerful coalitions. These determined women— with no voice of their own at the ballot box—lobbied successfully for the establishment of a state child welfare commission, child labor laws, a juvenile court system, public kindergartens, compulsory school attendance, pure food inspection, and a state library commission. At the same time, the Texas Association of Colored

Brownie, a fountain placed in Sam Houston Park in 1907 through joint efforts of the Civic Club and the city's school children, was a special friend to generations of young Houstonians. Brownie resides today at the Houston Zoo. (Photo by author)

The Houston Settlement Association was organized in 1907 in the home of Alice Graham Baker, who was elected president of the group. Mrs. Baker directed the Association's varied programs until 1918 when the settlement became part of the city's Social Service Bureau. (Courtesy James A. Baker III Family)

Children's activities were an integral part of Rusk Settlement. Here neighborhood children are enjoying an Easter egg hunt during the 1920s. (Franklin Harbach Collection, Houston Metropolitan Research Center, Houston Public Library)

Women's Clubs undertook extensive lobbying, which resulted in such projects as a home for delinquent girls.

As women moved from their parlors, they broadened their concerns into actions that made Houston a healthier, safer, more enlightened place. To accomplish this, they had to gain public acceptance for their programs, obtain financial support, and develop working coalitions. At the same time, they had to operate within the bounds of propriety, never forgetting their roles as homemakers. While they lacked power in the conventional sense, they were able to combine perseverance, intelligence, and an astute sense of timing to accomplish their goals.

Woman's sphere had expanded vastly.

Rusk Settlement conducted English classes for residents of the Second Ward. The Houston Settlement Association was among the earliest institutions in Houston to address the needs of the Mexican-American community. (Franklin Harbach Collection, Houston Metropolitan Research Center, Houston Public Library)

Story hour was eagerly awaited by children, who attended activities at the Rusk Settlement. Sybil Campbell, a staff member, is shown reading to the assembled group. (Houston Metropolitan Research Center, Houston Public Library)

Bethlehem Settlement opened in 1917 as an extension of the settlement house program. Activities at the Fourth Ward center included a nursery and kindergarten, boys' and girls' clubs, a mothers' club, a community chorus, and a playground—all planned and supervised by female volunteers until it closed in 1940. (Houston Metropolitan Research Center, Houston Public Library)

Julia Hester's home was known as one where children could come, whether it was for tutoring lessons, for a word of encouragement, or for a haven from the dangers of the street. In 1943 when the city opened its first community center in a black neighborhood, it was appropriately named for Julia Hester. Today Hester House remains an anchor of the Fifth Ward. (Houston Metropolitan Research Center, Houston Public Library)

In 1910 newspaper publisher Ferdie Trichelle founded the Emma R. News Boys Association. Club activities included woodworking classes, boxing matches, and dance lessons. At one point the membership numbered over four hundred. A facility was later opened to house some of the boys. In recognition of her efforts, Trichelle was appointed juvenile probation officer so that she could receive a salary from the city. (Elaine Finfrock Roberts Papers, Junior League Component, Houston Metropolitan Research Center, Houston Public Library)

The National Council of Jewish Women actively assisted immigrant women in their resettlement. The Houston section established the Working Girls' Home for low-salaried women, and sponsored job-training programs as well as English classes. Mrs. Maurice L. Goldman was not only active in the local group, but also served as president of the state organization. (Houston Metropolitan Research Center, Houston Public Library)

In 1923 a group of young women formed the Blue Bird Circle as a philanthropic organization to assist with local projects. Several years later they focused their efforts on funding and staffing a pediatric neurology clinic. Today the Blue Bird clinic is world-renowned as an exemplary medical facility. For more than sixty years, Blue Bird members have made and sold Easter baskets to raise funds. (Courtesy Blue Bird Circle)

Women's groups continually needed money for their projects. The Houston Heights Woman's Club had this carnival in 1911 to fund construction of its clubhouse. To benefit other projects it also sponsored theatrical performances. These were frequently produced and directed by Myrtle Cook Lowry, who graduated from home theatricals to become a nationally famous actress. (Courtesy Heights Branch Library, Houston Public Library)

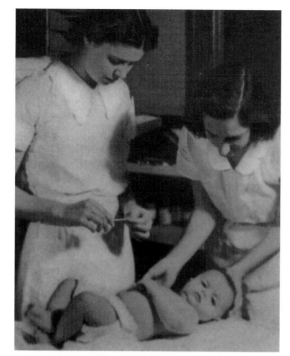

Two years after its founding in 1925, the Junior League of Houston opened a clinic in the basement of a downtown office building. When this photograph was made in 1940, services included examinations by physicians, infant care and first aid courses for new mothers, and a medical dispensary. Seventy-five years later the Junior League is still spearheading health care programs benefiting the entire community. (Courtesy Junior League of Houston)

In 1921 Frances Mann Law, who was serving as volunteer chairman of the City Recreation Department's playground committee, was asked to assist in organizing a Girl Scout troop. Within two years, five hundred girls were participating in twenty-four troops under the guidance of Commissioner Law, as she was called. (Houston Metropolitan Research Center, Houston Public Library)

Houston's female population always comprised a large volunteer corps for worthy causes. Sue Vaughan Clayton and Mary Gibbs Jones, shown here selling savings bonds during World War II, were frequently at the forefront of community projects. (Jesse Jones Collection, Houston Metropolitan Research Center, Houston Public Library)

In 1947 a group of women formed the Methodist Hospital Service Corps. Their purpose was to relieve nurses of duties which could be handled by trained volunteers. As the hospital grew in size, their roles expanded. Most local institutions today incorporate volunteers in their daily operations. (St. Luke's United Methodist Church Archives)

The Houston Junior Forum, a women's service group founded in 1946, recognized that many children in public schools did not have the skills needed to succeed in learning. Establishing libraries in schools where there were none, Forum members used storytelling and related activities—as seen here at Anson Jones School in 1951—to help young students improve their English and acquire a desire for learning. (Courtesy Houston Junior Forum)

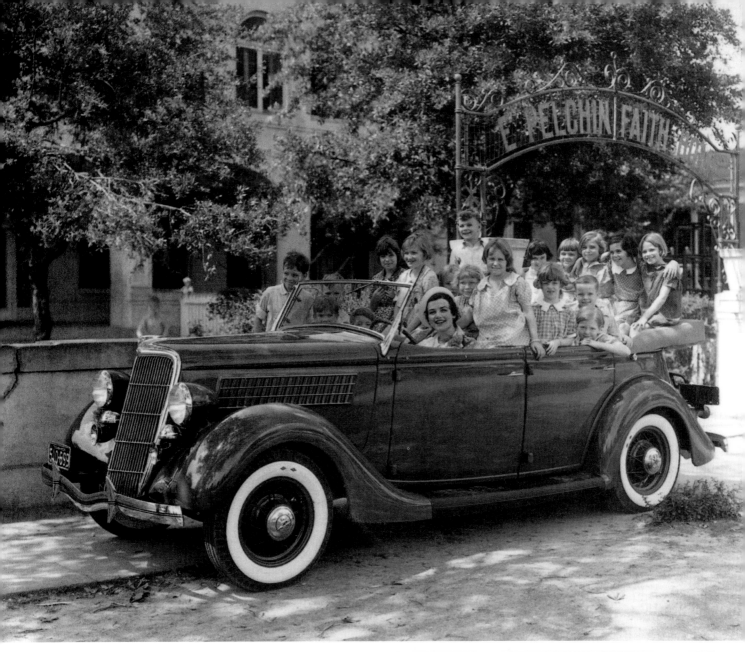

Women continued to be actively involved at Faith Home by sponsoring outings for the children, taking them to medical appointments, and seeing that daily needs were met. (Story Sloane's Gallery)

Women often formed clubs for pleasurable pursuits. Whist, a popular card game in the early twentieth century, provided not only social interaction but also stimulating mental activity. At the same time, the Study Whist Club met needs in the community by sewing for the children at Faith Home. (Houston Metropolitan Research Center, Houston Public Library)

Women's organizations became actively involved whenever there was a need in the community. Members of the South End Embroidery Club met regularly to roll bandages for the Red Cross during wartime. (Houston Metropolitan Research Center, Houston Public Library)

Garden clubs were organized in many neighborhoods to promote beautification and civic projects. The Monticello Garden Club, organized in 1936, focused on community landscaping and park improvements. (Courtesy of Rhea Scadden)

Wells Fargo & Company Express employed women in both clerical and secretarial positions. Its Houston office had a sizable female staff in 1915. (Houston Metropolitan Research Center, Houston Public Library)

CHAPTER IV

Going to Work

In August 1888 *The Ladies' Messenger*, a local publication, declared, "Every woman should be placed in such a position that she is independent. By all means see to it that they have . . . some means of winning their daily bread without dependence or charity." In strong contrast to the widely held view that the appropriate place for a woman was in her home, not in the public marketplace, *The Ladies' Messenger* was dedicated to promoting "women's thought and women's work." At this time, however, society still considered the successful woman to be a full-time homemaker.

Throughout American history women have done unpaid domestic work. They have cleaned their homes, cared for children, planted and harvested family gardens, cooked and served meals, and generally ministered to the physical and emotional needs of family members. Most often, their unpaid domestic chores have not been considered "work." Only when they have left home to earn wages have they been labeled working women. The nature of the work varied for women of different classes, races, and ethnic groups just as it changed with the increasing urbanization and industrialization of our society. What did not change were the constant tensions between two areas of women's lives: the home and the work place. Accordingly, a woman's position in the work force has often been controversial and gone unrecorded.

During Houston's early years, most women wage earners were domestic servants, laundresses, and seamstresses. The work had a low status and was largely invisible, since it was most often done in homes. There were, of course, exceptions to these traditional means of earning income. Pamelia Mann, an unusually independent woman who amassed considerable property in her own name, was operating the Mansion House hotel in Houston's busy commercial area as early as 1837. In another enterprising operation, Obedience Fort Smith formed a drayage service to move goods around town. At that time, however, most women who

Farms were a source of income for many families. Farm wives often produced marketable products by milking cows, raising chickens, and growing vegetables. (Houston Metropolitan Research Center, Houston Public Library)

worked to provide income did it unobtrusively and were almost anonymous in the process.

After the Civil War more women entered the work force. Yet female occupations were still limited primarily to domestic and caretaking roles. In 1877 the *Houston City Directory* revealed that most working women were engaged in running boarding houses, teaching school, sewing, and serving as domestics, although one saloon operator and a factory manager were listed. Clearly, many women needed to earn money to support themselves and their families.

A group of women who did not need to earn income themselves, but were nevertheless concerned about those who did, formed the Woman's Exchange in 1887. Part of a national movement, the local organization was made up of middle-class women who paid monthly dues of twenty-five-cents. It operated as an informal agency for female employment and served as a commission house selling women's handmade goods—from fancy and plain sewing to edible delicacies. Since sewing was a marketable skill, the Woman's Exchange conducted sewing classes for young girls, hoping to increase their potential as wage earners. Although the Woman's

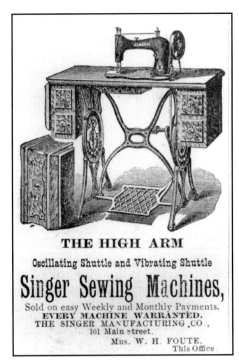

The sewing machine was probably the most significant labor-saving device in the late nineteenth century, benefiting both housewives and wage-earning seamstresses. When this advertisement appeared in *The Ladies' Messenger* in 1887, however, models were still a luxury for many families. It was not uncommon for women to share a machine with friends, thus making it a more affordable household item. (Houston Metropolitan Research Center, Houston Public Library)

In the late nineteenth century, most female retailers in Houston ran fancy goods stores which specialized in fabric, buttons, ribbons, and such ready-made apparel as corsets, gloves, and hosiery. These stores, frequently combined with millinery or dressmaking establishments, catered to a predominantly female clientele. (*1885 Directory for the City of Houston*, Houston Public Library)

Exchange limited its scope of involvement—minority women were apparently not included in its efforts—it continued for several years, despite the social prejudices against female employment, as a means of offering women a way to supplement their family incomes.

During the last two decades of the nineteenth century an increasing number of women became business owners. Their businesses were typically enterprises which utilized domestic skills and required little start-up capital. Women opened restaurants and confectioneries, laundries and grocery stores, rooming houses and beauty parlors, millinery shops and fancy goods stores. Women like Mrs. E. H. Nitze, Mrs. A. Bentley, and Miss M. A. Zwieb advertised their businesses to the general public although their offerings were directed largely to a female clientele. Many of these women, with or without formal schooling, had moved from apprentice to employee to independent entrepreneur.

Because severe restraints were imposed on any married woman who considered establishing a business, female entrepreneurs were most often widows or spinsters. While a single woman—legally termed a *feme sole*—could freely engage in business transactions, the *feme covert* status of a married woman allowed her, when establishing a business, to use only her separate property usually acquired before marriage. This status also precluded her from utilizing any profits from the business in its operation, since such profits were community property controlled by her husband. Additionally, she was also prohibited from signing contracts.

By the 1890s educated women or those with means to pay for business courses found new employment opportunities in office work.

Women often owned grocery stores, businesses in which they dealt primarily with female customers. Sarah Goolsby was the proprietor of this store in the 1920s. (Houston Metropolitan Research Center, Houston Public Library)

Many women utilized their domestic skills by operating boarding houses. Some merely rented extra rooms in their home while others, like Pauline Rosenfield, ran sizable establishments. (Mrs. Ben Blum Papers, Junior League Component, Houston Metropolitan Research Center, Houston Public Library)

Eciquia Castro, a well-known purveyor of Mexican food in the city, owned a cafe in the Fourth Ward in the early twentieth century. (Castro Family Collection, Houston Metropolitan Research Center, Houston Public Library)

Schools such as Draughon's Business College attracted large numbers of females eager to learn skills required for employment in offices. (Houston Metropolitan Research Center, Houston Public Library)

In 1910 Stewart Abstract and Title Co. had females in the positions of stenographer and typist. By 1920, eighty-seven percent of all secretarial jobs in Texas were held by women. (Houston Metropolitan Research Center, Houston Public Library)

Business schools began training women as stenographers, bookkeepers, or "typewriters," who were given the same name as the recently invented machines. There was a widespread belief that such female traits as manual dexterity, attention to minor details, and talents as caretakers made them particularly suited to office work. Although the workday was long—usually about ten hours—the work itself was in a respectable setting, and the wages were relatively good. As they graduated from high school in Houston, an increasing number of young women began working in offices.

Another technological improvement, the telephone, also opened a new field of employment for women. The number of telephones needed by Houston's expanding population soared, and telephone operating was soon defined as a woman's field. It became an acceptable job for women because it was carefully supervised, offered no undesirably close association with male employees, did not require burdensome physical labor, and

screened the women from public view. Despite the occupation's gentility, conditions were poor and wages were low. For working a nine-hour shift seven days a week, operators received $15 and were allowed no sick leave. To remedy this situation, the operators went on strike in July 1900—the first such incident in the city to involve women. As a result, some improvements were made in benefits and working conditions for the "hello girls," as they were popularly called.

Retail clerking was another occupation that opened to women. Stores actively recruited well-mannered women who could deal comfortably with customers. Although the prospect of working in a department store like Levy's, Foley's or Mistrot-Munn appealed to some women, the work was in reality arduous and wages were low— about $3.50 a week. Saleswomen stood behind the counter for twelve or more hours a day. Few stores permitted their saleswomen to sit down during business hours, and some clerks fainted from exhaustion.

Houston's reform-minded club women banded together to address

In 1915 Estella B. Jackson became the first female notary public in Harris County. She later became manager of A. G. Perkins and Company, which handled land, loan, and legal business. (Houston Metropolitan Research Center, Houston Public Library)

When this telephone exchange opened in 1910, working conditions had improved for the company's operators. Days were shorter, wages were higher, and new facilities included refreshment rooms and rooftop areas where workers could escape from the heat of the switchboard room. (Houston Metropolitan Research Center, Houston Public Library)

This book and stationery store on Main Street offered employment to women in 1910. Although the hours were often long, clerking was considered a suitable female occupation; and these jobs were eagerly sought. (Houston Metropolitan Research Center, Houston Public Library)

these harsh conditions. Through boycotting those businesses that refused to institute more humane practices, they were eventually able to persuade store owners to lower the mandatory work hours and to allow rest breaks with suitable seating. Recognizing another inadequacy, a group of women organized for the express purpose of providing a restroom in the Market House for rural women who came into Houston to sell their farm products. Not until 1918 were there any statutory requirements for separate restrooms.

While new opportunities became available to some Houston women, others were still confined to domestic jobs. Black women worked long hours and received low pay as housekeepers, office cleaners, maids, cooks, or hotel chambermaids. Immigrant women most often found employment as factory workers. In 1911 there were six thousand women—a fourth of the city's entire industrial force—working in factories, especially in the garment trade. Despairing of their twelve-hour work days in unhealthy surroundings, female garment workers formed a labor union—the only

Working conditions in commercial laundries were generally poor. Despite consant standing on cement floors; high temperatures with poor ventilation; inadequate toilet facilities; and no lunch rooms, rest areas, drinking cups, or safety equipment, these jobs were often the only ones available for many women. (Houston Metropolitan Research Center, Houston Public Library)

Women worked long hours to produce jams and preserves in a fig factory near Aldine. Though the fruit was received neatly boxed, the actual production took place under highly undesirable conditions. (Houston Metropolitan Research Center, Houston Public Library)

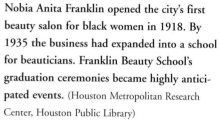

Nobia Anita Franklin opened the city's first beauty salon for black women in 1918. By 1935 the business had expanded into a school for beauticians. Franklin Beauty School's graduation ceremonies became highly anticipated events. (Houston Metropolitan Research Center, Houston Public Library)

Black beauticians went to the homes of their white clients in wealthy neighborhoods until they were forced by a white beauticians' association to stop. Beauty shops for black clientele were then opened with some featuring Turkish baths and trained masseuses. (Houston Metropolitan Research Center, Houston Public Library)

Annie Hagen (shown here with her family), was considered one of the best midwives in her community. Trained by local doctors, Mrs. Hagen qualified for an Experienced Trained Nurses Certificate and organized the Trained Nurses Club. (Houston Metropolitan Research Center, Houston Public Library)

In 1894 Irene McBride became the first postmaster for the Houston Heights. She served in the position for three years during which the postal facilities were located at the McBride's store, the first to be established in the Heights. (Houston Metropolitan Research Center, Houston Public Library)

one in the city comprised of women. By unionizing they hoped to coerce management into improving their working conditions.

In 1913 Houstonian Eva Goldsmith, president of the state garment workers' union, was the star lobbyist in forcing the passage of legislation which limited the work of women in industry to fifty-four hours per week, with a maximum of ten hours per day. Thus, labor activism enabled working-class women to assume a public role that middle-class women had already perfected—legislative lobbying.

Houston's work force always included both married and single women, but its unmarried women greatly outnumbered wives and mothers. Married women usually worked only when forced by economic necessity to supplement the marginal wages earned by their husbands. Many single women employed outside the home considered their work a temporary source of livelihood before marriage. Immigrant daughters worked to contribute to the meager incomes of their families. An increasing number of migrant women came from rural areas for the promising economic opportunities provided in Houston.

It was these "women adrift," as the newcomers to the city were known, whose safety and welfare caused concern in the community. On January 26, 1907, a meeting was held in Houston to organize Texas' first branch of the Young Women's Christian Association. Not only did the YWCA establish a residence which provided affordable and morally safe living quarters for these workers, but it also furnished a downtown facility that had a lunch room, gymnasium, and restrooms with couches and reading materials. A variety of free lectures was held. A popular one was on hygiene, demonstrating the importance of physical activity for young ladies closely confined in offices. Realizing that legislation was the ultimate solution in improving conditions for employed women, the YWCA, which by 1912 claimed fourteen hundred Houston women as members, was visibly active in promoting laws to regulate wages and hours.

During the 1920s larger numbers of Houston women entered the work force although the range of jobs remained narrow. Women's work was still characterized by low pay, long hours, and few opportunities for advancement. Even as clerical positions for women increased, the route to management was closed. With the exception of teaching, most white-collar jobs were off-limits to black women. Hispanic women had few choices other than as domestic servants or factory workers.

During the Great Depression a few women were given jobs through federal work-relief programs in sewing rooms, cafeterias, hospitals, and nursery schools while others cleaned public buildings and worked in canning factories. Local artists were employed by the government to decorate public buildings. Women, however, often lost their jobs during the depression because it was considered essential that men occupy any available positions other than those characterized as "women's work." Many women, desperate to earn money, turned to prostitution or to low-paying domestic service.

With the outbreak of World War II all this changed. Indeed, women were urged to work as a patriotic duty in order to keep the war economy booming. To attract women into wartime industries, the War Manpower Commission created "Rosie the Riveter" as a symbol of female employment. Posters featuring Rosie filled billboards and sides of buildings, as well as newspapers and magazines. Women readily found work in war-related industries where they earned an average of $40 per week—considerably more than previous jobs had paid them. Many worked in aircraft plants. Others—welders, draftswomen, and machinists—built warships. Women also worked in such industries as steel mills and oil refineries as replacements for men who had entered the military. Females soon comprised half of this work force. The Office of War Information noted that war production work had "disproved the old bugaboo that women have no mechanical ability and that they are a distracting influence in industry."

In 1924 newspaper reporter Elizabeth Minor Welch was lauded by local judges for her coverage of the courthouse beat for the *Houston Post*. She had begun her journalistic career as war correspondent at Camp Logan in 1917, using the name of E. C. Minor to conceal the fact that she was a woman. After successful stints with other papers, she was hired by the *Post* as a staff reporter. (Houston Metropolitan Research Center, Houston Public Library)

Many women joined the workforce as waitresses. Among the most visible in Houston were the carhops at Prince's drive-ins. For more than forty years they served the motoring public and became legendary in the process. (Houston Metropolitan Research Center, Houston Public Library)

For $2.50 to $3.75 a week Houston's YWCA provided affordable living facilities for working women, and served as a safe haven for social activities. The local organization, which recorded a membership of fourteen hundred in 1912, opened a new field of employment to women by creating specialized positions in its own operations. In 1918 the Blue Triangle Branch of the YWCA was founded for black women. It also established a residence and an activity center, as well as a Galveston Bay campsite. (Houston Metropolitan Research Center, Houston Public Library)

In 1912 ground was broken for the Young Women's Co-operative Home, a project of the Methodist Woman's Board of City Missions. The home, which offered low-cost housing for working women, emphasized its amenities: a library, a social hall equipped with a grand piano and victrola, and parlors for entertaining friends. (Houston Metropolitan Research Center, Houston Public Library)

Women entered every part of military service except combat. They joined the Women's Airforce Service Pilots (WASP), the Women's Army Corps (WAC), and Women Accepted for Voluntary Emergency Services (WAVES). While most served in administrative, clerical, and communications jobs, some women pilots received training at Houston's Ellington Field in ferrying aircraft, towing targets for gunnery practice, and transporting cargo and personnel. Houstonian Oveta Culp Hobby, director of the Women's Army Corps, proclaimed, "Women are carrying on the glorious tradition of American womanhood. They are making history!"

When the war ended, the vast majority of women who worked for wages during the conflict wanted to keep their jobs. Instead, they usually lost them to returning veterans. Although the war helped women's work become an increasingly accepted part of middle-class life, a large segment of society still regarded working women with disapproval.

Nevertheless, the rate of female employment accelerated during the post-war years. Between 1960 and 1980 the female workforce almost doubled. In a quest for higher living standards, many married women took

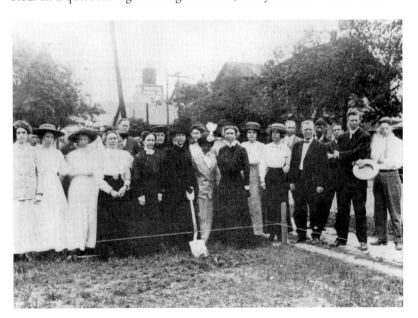

Women in the business community frequently formed organizations to advance their common interest and to perform community service. Club Femenino Chapultepec, comprised of unmarried Mexican American women, began in 1931 as part of the Business and Professional Department of the YWCA.
(Gomez Family Collection, Houston Metropolitan Research Center, Houston Public Library)

jobs to provide second incomes for their families. Educational opportunities for females expanded, and federal legislation impacted female employment by addressing issues of gender equality. As a result, women became insurance adjusters, bus drivers, construction workers, firefighters, television newscasters—all jobs previously relegated to men. They also began to fill management positions, especially in banking and finance, business, and government. In 1983 women's work rose to new heights when astronaut Sally Ride soared into outer space.

Houston women have long been part of the paid labor force. Not only has their work been essential to the functioning of the city, but it has also been integral to its economy. That reality will doubtless continue into the twenty-first century.

Realizing that women enjoyed competing in athletics, many businesses sponsored teams for their female employees. The Great Southern Life Company basketball team is shown in 1927. (Houston Metropolitan Research Center, Houston Public Library)

One of the city's earliest business clubs for females was the Women's Advertising Club, organized in 1925. They are shown here on a bus trip designed to stimulate interest in beautifying Buffalo Bayou. (Houston Metropolitan Research Center, Houston Public Library)

Mollie Bailey's Circus, frequently billed as the only one in the world owned by a woman, traveled Texas for thirty years. The circus wintered in Houston each year. When spring came, the magic cry in small towns all over the state was, "Aunt Mollie's coming!" (Dallas Historical Society www.dallashist.org)

A member of one of Houston's wealthiest families, Ella Hutchins Stewart Sydnor lived amid wealth and privilege. This lifestyle, however, did not exclude her participation in business. Between 1890 and 1900 she and Corra Bacon Foster were partners in the real estate firm, Foster and Stewart. During this time the business partners were the only female members of the Houston Cotton Exchange and Board of Trade. (Houston Metropolitan Research Center, Houston Public Library)

After serving more than fifteen years as editor of the *Railroad Echo*, a newspaper for railroad employees, Ferdie Trichelle began a new business when she formed Tri-Fin Oil Operators. She and her partner, Alice Finfrock, brought in their first gusher on April 17, 1922. (Elaine Finfrock Roberts Papers, Junior League Component, Houston Metropolitan Research Center, Houston Public Library)

Teal Portrait Studio operated for more than forty years. Although Elnora Teal developed her photographic skills under her husband's tutelage, she eventually ran the firm's main studio. Photography by Mrs. Teal, who was widely acclaimed because of her close attention to detail, can be found today in many Texas research centers. (Houston Metropolitan Research Center, Houston Public Library)

The Ritz Theater was built by Kate Scanlan in 1926. An astute businesswoman, she and her sisters had earlier constructed the ten-story Scanlan Building as a memorial to their father. Both of these structures are standing today. (Photo by author)

After the death of her husband, Mellie Keenan Esperson took control of his interests in oil, ranching, and industrial development. In 1927 she erected the Niels Esperson Building. She is shown here entertaining business associates on her private terrace atop the structure. (Houston Metropolitan Research Center, Houston Public Library)

Women joined the work force in large numbers during World War II and were accepted for the first time in such jobs as machining rock bit cones at Hughes Tool Company. One permanent result of expanded female employment was improved conditions in the workplace. (Hughes Tool Company Collection, Houston Metropolitan Research Center, Houston Public Library)

As one of the first women in Houston real estate development, Katherine B. Mott began building speculative homes in the late 1920s. Her homes were noted for good planning, fine craftsmanship, and distinctive design. She built this one in River Oaks for her own family. (Photo by author)

As the first director of the Women's Army Corps, Oveta Culp Hobby commanded more than 100,000 women during World War II. By the end of the war, women were filling 239 army jobs. For her outstanding contributions, Colonel Hobby was awarded the **Distinguished Service Medal.** (Houston Metropolitan Research Center, Houston Public Library)

The WASPs (Women's Airforce Service Pilots) flew sixty million miles during World War II as they ferried war planes, towed targets for gunnery practice, and tested aircraft. **Not until 1977 were surviving WASPs granted retirement benefits by Congress.** (UT Institute of Texan Cultures at San Antonio, courtesy U.S. Air Force)

Anita Martini, a pioneer among women sports journalists, was the first female sports anchor in the nation and was the first woman granted access to a major league team's locker room. During her twenty-five-year broadcasting career she was a strong voice for equal opportunities for male and female sports journalists. (*Houston Chronicle*)

Marcella Donovan Perry achieved prominence as she built Heights Savings Association into a leading financial institution. Active in many civic endeavors, Perry was the first woman to serve on the Houston Chamber of Commerce Board and was the first female member of the Port Commission. (Courtesy of Gayle Perry Saunders; photograph by Gittings)

In 1983 Dr. Sally Ride became the first U.S. woman in space, orbiting earth 231 times. Today females are found in every area of the space program. (Courtesy National Aeronautics and Space Administration)

Angelina Morales, the first female funeral director and embalmer in Harris County, participated in the operation of a family-owned funeral home for sixty years. Morales, along with her husband, pioneered in another industry, radio broadcasting, by establishing in 1950 KLVL, the Texas gulf coast's first Hispanic radio station. (Houston Metropolitan Research Center, Houston Public Library)

Annette Finnigan, an 1894 graduate of Wellesley College, credited her experience at Wellesley, an all-female school with an all-female faculty, with giving her a strong academic education and a thorough grounding in developing the leadership qualities that she would later put to good use.

(Finnigan Collection, Houston Metropolitan Research Center, Houston Public Library)

CHAPTER V

Expanding Education

An unusual event occurred at Wellesley College in the spring of 1894. The commencement exercises included a young woman from Texas. Her name was Annette Finnigan. At a time when only two percent of the nation's females attended college, Finnigan's achievement was unique. She had received her early education in Houston schools; and after spending a year at Tilden Seminary in New Hampshire, she entered Wellesley. The Finnigan family, who placed a high priority on education, made sure that Annette and her two sisters had the same educational opportunities then offered to males. Her studies prepared her for a life that would include business affairs, political activism, and philanthropy.

Annette Finnigan's experience reflected a changing trend in women's education. Early female educators—although aware of society's expectation that the role of women would be governed by the precepts of piety, purity, domesticity, and submission—had insisted that learning was also essential. In the years following the Civil War, defenders of higher education for women argued that society had an obligation to educate women as full human beings, and that females did indeed have the mental and physical capacity for higher education.

This expansion of education altered the lives of many females. The period between girlhood and marriage became a time in which women could enter a variety of pursuits, including higher education. As a result, colleges began opening their doors to women. The University of Texas was coeducational from its beginning in 1883. Baylor University had periodically admitted female students from its founding in 1845, although women attended separate classes and received degrees different from those awarded to males, one example being Mistress of Polite Literature. By 1892, however, women and men at Baylor were offered the same courses and received the same degrees. With the opening of numerous teacher-training institutions like Prairie View State Normal and Industrial

This portrait of Mary B. Cross was probably taken for her graduation from Prairie View State Normal and Industrial College about 1909 when half of the school's graduates were women. Their major subjects were sewing, millinery, cooking, dairying, and normal school courses; but they also studied Latin, Greek, civics, and geometry. (Houston Metropolitan Research Center, Houston Public Library)

College—now Prairie View A&M University—and the establishment of the Girls' Industrial College—now Texas Woman's University—the availability of higher education greatly increased for women.

Most women attending college in the late nineteenth century were from middle-class families. Poorer families could not afford the expense of a college education; and wealthy Houstonians favored educating daughters privately at home, in boarding schools, and through travel abroad. Going to college was an unusual and complicated process for native white women who were considered social rebels for wanting higher education.

Aspiring women from black and foreign-born families found the route even more difficult. However, by World War I attitudes began to change, and collegiate education attracted women of many backgrounds.

After their years at college, some women were far too committed to the pursuit of knowledge or the practical application of their education to retreat willingly to the narrow confines of Victorian domesticity. Between 1890 and 1920 women made their entry into the professions. These early pioneers proved that females were capable of the highest intellectual achievement, that they were physically able to meet the demands of long hours and strenuous work, and that they had the drive and tenacity to stick to their callings.

Women had worked as teachers before higher education became a prerequisite. As teaching became professionalized, however, a college degree and certification were required. As females met these requirements, they quickly became the majority of elementary and secondary school-teachers. When a single teacher married, however, she was forced to

When Rice Institute opened in 1912, seventeen young women enrolled in the first class. All courses were open to females and males alike. The Institute received criticism for not offering "women's courses," such as home economics, art, and pedagogy. The women themselves, however, voiced no objections. Eleven of the original female enrollees graduated four years later. (Woodson Research Center, Fondren Library, Rice University)

resign—a policy that remained in effect in the Houston school system for many years.

Women's entry into teaching on the college level was much slower. Although women were admitted into some graduate programs in the late nineteenth century, they remained few in number until the 1920s. William Marsh Rice Institute—now Rice University—conferred its first Ph.D. on a female student in 1929. Women who earned graduate degrees found that faculty appointments were difficult to obtain due to fears in the academic community that the profession might become "feminized." Still, however, women continued to pursue graduate degrees in order to teach in universities and colleges. Today they comprise one-third of the faculties in Houston area institutions of higher learning.

Women also dominated nursing as it began to establish itself as a profession. Women had traditionally tended to their families, friends, and neighbors. The Civil War had utilized the services of many volunteer nurses, although these services were as much menial and domestic as medical. Unlike doctors, nurses were not required to have professional train-

In the early twentieth century physical activities became part of a woman's course of study in educational institutions. These students at Houston College are being instructed in calisthenics. (Houston Metropolitan Research Center, Houston Public Library)

The faculty of Sherman School in 1914 was almost entirely female. A beginning teacher's salary at that time ranged from $45 to $90 per month, depending on the grade level. Although women filled most teaching positions, very few advanced to administrative posts. (Houston Metropolitan Research Center, Houston Public Library)

ing. Nevertheless, by the early twentieth century, nursing schools were established. Catholic orders supplied the first trained nurses in Texas. These nurses staffed numerous hospitals, one of them being Houston's St. Joseph's Infirmary.

In 1907 Baptist Sanitarium opened a nursing school in Houston. Its program was designed to equip young women students with the skills, strength of character, and perseverance to withstand the rigors of a life in which they were expected to wash bedpans, change beds, roll bandages, clean patients' rooms, prepare meals, keep records, follow doctors' orders without question, and boil syringes, surgical instruments, and gloves. In spite of the demanding work and twelve-hour days, nursing became the bridge by which women extended their traditional domestic role of caring for the sick into the public world of work.

While women were encouraged to enter the profession of nursing, they fought an uphill battle to become doctors. Frequently, they met opposition similar to that expressed in an 1853 publication: "FOR MYSELF, I prefer prescriptions written by a masculine hand; shan't submit my pulse to anything that wears a bonnet!" The American Medical

Teacher Pinky Yates is shown in 1910 with her class at Colored High School in Houston's Fourth Ward. In the segregated school system, teachers in black schools received less salary than their counterparts in white schools. Not until 1943 were salaries equalized. (Jack Yates Collection, Houston Metropolitan Research Center, Houston Public Library)

Association three years later recommended barring women from medical schools while instituting a system of licensing to ensure that only graduates in medicine could become practicing physicians. By 1860, recognizing that women had unique nurturing and healing abilities, a few medical schools for women were opened, but none were located in Texas. Houston's first female physicians were, therefore, trained in out-of-state institutions. However, by 1894 the University of Texas Medical Branch at Galveston graduated its first woman and continued to graduate an average of one every second year until 1920.

During the early years of the twentieth century, Houston could claim a growing number of women who were medical pioneers. Minnie Clifton Archer, a familiar figure who made her rounds in one of the first electric coupes in town, established a practice in her specialty—eye, ear, nose, and throat—and in 1898 she became the first female member of the Texas Medical Society. Lithuanian-born Ray Karchmer Daily began practicing ophthalmology in 1914. She was recognized as a leader when she became the first woman president of Memorial Hospital's medical staff in 1932 and was later selected as chief of staff at Jefferson Davis, the city's charity hospital. During the Depression years, Ruth Hartgraves boarded a train for Boston carrying a shoe box full of sandwiches, one suitcase, and five dollars in cash. After serving a hard-earned internship in that city and completing her residency in New York, she returned to Houston to practice obstetrics and gynecology. A distinguishing characteristic of her practice was a spotlight mounted on her car. She found this to be a useful tool as she looked for homes of patients who frequently called to have babies delivered in the middle of the night.

Other female physicians moved into the field of public health. Tuberculosis, a prevalent and often-fatal disease in the early years of the twentieth century, caught the attention of Elva Anis Wright, who founded the Houston and Harris County Anti-Tuberculosis League in 1908. For the next forty years, Dr. Wright dedicated her life to the detection and prevention of this disease, especially in children.

Today females in Houston comprise about a fourth of the city's physicians and can be found practicing in almost every medical specialty, teaching in medical schools, and conducting important research.

The legal profession was even less accessible to women than the medical. In 1873 the United States Supreme Court opined that "the natural and proper timidity and delicacy" of women rendered them unfit to practice law. Before 1870 most lawyers learned their trade though apprenticeship, and a few women in families of lawyers were encouraged by fathers, husbands, or brothers to read law books and to master the material. When law schools were established, however, women were usually excluded from them. Even after women were fully accepted—the University of Texas Law School graduated its first female in 1914—they discovered that most state bars would not admit them and that law firms were reluctant to hire them. In 1910 the federal census listed only three female attorneys in Texas.

One of the three was Hortense Sparks Ward. Ward, after first working as a court reporter, had studied law through correspondence courses and became the first woman in Texas to

In 1917 Mabel Wesley became principal of Crawford Elementary School. With a faculty of nineteen, it was then the state's largest public school headed by a woman. Mrs. Wesley remained principal until her death in 1941. Today Wesley Elementary School is named for this pioneer educator. (Photo by author)

The Kinkaid School
Faculty
1921

In 1906 Margaret Kinkaid opened a school in her home with seven students. By 1921 the faculty was instructing 125 boys and girls under the direction of Mrs. Kinkaid (shown on the right). Kinkaid School continues to educate young Houstonians. (Courtesy of Pat Jumonville)

pass the bar examination. She then joined her husband in his Houston law office. Although she was admitted to practice before the United States Supreme Court and in all Texas courts, Ward never made court appearances, fearing that her presence might prejudice juries, which in Texas were exclusively male until 1954. Ward limited her work to consultations and to writing briefs. A unique incident of her career occurred in 1925 when she was named chief justice of an all-woman Supreme Court appointed by the governor to hear a single case in which all the male judges had to disqualify themselves.

This event, however, did not mark the beginning of women's movement into the judiciary. Forty-eight years would pass before a woman would occupy a judicial bench in Harris County. In 1973 Ruby Sondock was appointed to a domestic relations court, making her the first and only woman judge in Houston until 1977 when Joe Kegans became the first woman in Texas to serve on a criminal court bench. In Houston today, women can be found as judges in municipal, county, state, and federal courts.

Despite the prevalence and importance of female members in most churches, women were even less welcome in the ministry than in medicine or law. Neither Catholics, Jews, nor mainstream Protestants permitted female clergy. By the end of the nineteenth century, only a tiny handful of women in the entire country had been ordained. This trend did not significantly change until the late 1950s when some religious bodies began accepting women as ministers, priests, and rabbis. Although the enroll-

Many women made teaching a lifetime job. Genevieve Johnson began her career at Fannin School. Known by her students as Miss Genevieve, she was named dean of the city's first junior high school when it opened in 1914. She held the position for many years. (Houston Metropolitan Research Center, Houston Public Library)

Public school teachers were at the core of black professionals in the early twentieth century. Mollie Brown taught for years at Douglass School in Houston's Third Ward, where this photograph was taken circa 1906–11. (Houston Metropolitan Research Center, Houston Public Library)

ment in many theological seminaries today is one-third female, the number of ordained women in Houston remains quite small.

At the turn of the century women led in the creation of a new profession, library science. As public libraries, and especially their services for children, expanded to keep pace with the growing urban population, so did the need for an educated but low-paid staff. Women, long regarded as the genteel caretakers of culture and children, filled that need. Houston's first public library opened in 1904 with a predominantly female staff under the direction of head librarian Julia Ideson, who had received her training at the University of Texas. During her forty-year tenure, Ideson effected many policies that further professionalized the field of library science.

Rooted in the tradition of women's sectarian charity, the profession of social work also emerged at the beginning of the twentieth century. Women's activities on behalf of the welfare of underprivileged members of the community began as a volunteer effort. The settlement house movement had provided a growing sense of professionalism to the many programs which evolved from its activities. By 1920 the volunteer worker was being replaced by the trained, salaried employee—most frequently in a government agency. Social work was no longer considered merely an extension of "woman's sphere," as it had been for over a century. Instead, it was viewed as a viable new profession for women.

The expansion of educational opportunities has had a profound influence on women. While many have used their education in a wide range of occupations and professions, a great many others have elected to make effective use of their learning in familial roles and community volunteerism. Whatever the choice, education has changed women's lives.

In return, learned women have contributed—and continue to contribute—significantly to our society.

Dr. Marguerite Ross Barnett became one of the first black women to be president of a major U.S. university when she was appointed to the University of Houston position in 1990. She served until her death in 1992. (Special Collections and Archives, University of Houston Libraries)

Women became more involved in higher education when they began serving on university boards. The University of Houston's first Board of Regents after its admission to the state system of higher education is pictured in 1963 with Lyndall Finley Wortham as its only female member. Mrs. Wortham served on the board for sixteen years. (Special Collections and Archives, University of Houston Libraries)

In 1887 Sisters of Charity of the Incarnate Word opened St. Joseph's Infirmary in a deserted frame house in downtown Houston. They became known as nurses of mercy as disease frequently ravaged the city. Today Christus St. Joseph Hospital continues the Sisters' mission of healing. (Houston Metropolitan Research Center, Houston Public Library)

In 1905 Ida J. Rudisill opened a private sanitarium. When she sold it two years later, it became the second Baptist hospital in the nation and Mrs. Rudisill was named the hospital's first superintendent of nursing. Houston's Memorial Healthcare System—now Memorial Hermann—emerged from those early efforts.
(Courtesy Memorial Hermann Southwest Hospital)

Lillie Jolly became Superintendent of Nurses at Baptist Sanitarium and Nursing School in 1922. By the time she retired in 1947, more than nine hundred nurses had graduated under her supervision. The Lillie Jolly School of Nursing, as it was named in 1945, was later incorporated into Houston Baptist University.
(McGovern Center, Texas Medical Center Library)

MRS. ROBT. JOLLY, DIRECTOR OF NURSING,
CONDUCTING CONFERENCE
MEMORIAL HOSPITAL HOUSTON 5-8-36.

There were few opportunities for black women in Texas to study nursing until 1918 when Prairie View College of Nursing was opened. In 1931 Houston Negro Hospital—now Riverside General Hospital—opened a nursing school. Although it existed for only a few years, it promoted nursing as a viable career for black women. (Houston Metropolitan Research Center, Houston Public Library)

The U.S. Cadet Nurses Corps was established during World War II to give a boost to nursing education. These women graduated in 1944 from The Methodist Hospital's program. (Courtesy The Methodist Hospital)

Josie M. Roberts joined The Methodist Hospital staff as chief clerk in 1924. She was elevated to the position of superintendent in 1932 and served for twenty-one years, guiding the hospital in its unprecedented growth. During much of this time, another woman, Marguerite Bright, was the administrator of Houston Negro Hospital. (Courtesy The Methodist Hospital)

After graduating from Woman's Medical College in Chicago in 1871, Margaret Ellen Holland established her practice in Houston, becoming the city's first female physician. Recognizing the importance of education, Dr. Holland became a leader in the Public School Art League and the local Parent-Teacher Association.
(Houston Metropolitan Research Center, Houston Public Library)

After being refused admittance to Yale and Harvard because she was a woman, Ray Karchmer Daily graduated at the top of her class from the University of Texas Medical Branch at Galveston in 1913. Two years later, she was the only female physician among the founders of the Houston Academy of Medicine. (Moody Medical Library, University of Texas Medical Branch, Galveston)

During her fifty-year career, Ruth Hartgraves won many awards for her contributions to medicine. One of her personal goals was to open doors for young women entering the medical field. Accordingly, Dr. Hartgraves endowed a chair at the University of Texas Medical Branch in Galveston, where she graduated in 1932. (McGovern Center, Texas Medical Center Library)

Dr. Elva Anis Wright established the first clinic for children at the City Health Department, where she advocated courses in pre-natal care and infant welfare. Dr. Wright was a strong proponent of quality health care for all children, regardless of their families' economic status. (McGovern Center, Texas Medical Center Library)

During her forty-five-year career in medicine, Violet Keiller's microscope was always by her side. Dr. Keiller was known for being readily available to demonstrate surgical and clinical pathology to students, interns, and residents in her midst. A pathology lab at Hermann Hospital bears her name today. (McGovern Center, Texas Medical Center Library)

Dr. Thelma Patten Law, one of the state's first black female physicians, began practicing in Houston in 1923. During her long career she was an active member of the Lone Star State Medical Association.
(McGovern Center, Texas Medical Center Library)

As a psychiatrist, Hilda Bruch worked with adolescents who had eating disorders. This led to the publication of her numerous writings on anorexia nervosa. As a professor at Baylor College of Medicine, Dr. Bruch received many awards in recognition of her written and clinical contributions to American psychiatric thought.
(McGovern Center, Texas Medical Center Library)

Native Houstonian Catherine Roett received her medical degree from Howard University in 1946. She began her career as a pediatrician in the clinics of Jefferson Davis Hospital, making her the first black pediatrician in the city. (McGovern Center, Texas Medical Center Library)

Mildred Grambling Dupuis was one of the first women in Texas to be licensed as a pharmacist. Following her certification in 1924, Dupuis and her husband operated Yale Pharmacy, where she practiced pharmacy for more than sixty years. (Courtesy Joe Dupuis)

Alice Jane Drysdale Sheffield was one of the earliest female graduates of the University of Texas Law School. A newspaper article at the time commended her for her stamina in pursuing the study of law. After becoming a licensed attorney in 1918, she joined the legal department of Gulf Oil Corporation, where she had a long and distinguished career. (St. Luke's United Methodist Church Archives)

In 1925 members of the specially appointed all-woman Texas Supreme Court, of which Houstonian Hortense Ward was Chief Justice, issued a ruling in the case of *Johnson v. Darr*. It is a matter of record that the female justices did not raise their hands to take the oath of office, perhaps feeling that such an action was unladylike. (UT Institute of Texan Cultures at San Antonio, courtesy of Garson Jackson)

Upon graduating from the University of Texas Law School in 1926, Joyce Burg was told that law was not a "woman's place." Unable to find a position in Houston, she moved to New York City. After returning to Houston in 1933, she opened the first female law partnership in Texas and soon thereafter formed a professional organization for female lawyers in Houston. Burg practiced until she was ninety-five. (Courtesy Houston Bar Association)

Billye N. Russell graduated from Houston Law School and opened a solo practice in 1932. Russell protested male dominance of the Houston Bar Association until finally a woman was named to its board in 1952. Forty years later the Houston Bar Association elected its first female president. (Courtesy Houston Bar Association)

In 1979 Gabrielle McDonald became the first woman to serve as a judge of the United States District Court for the Southern District of Texas. (*Houston Chronicle*)

The Reverend Helen M. Havens is shown celebrating the Holy Eucharist at Christ Church Cathedral during the International Women's Year Observance in 1977. Havens had been ordained to the priesthood earlier that year, making her one of the first Houston women to receive full ordination from a religious body. (Courtesy Helen M. Havens)

The staff of the Houston Lyceum and Carnegie Library is pictured on the steps of the library about 1910. Two of the librarians, Julia Ideson and Martha Schnitzer, each had careers of more than four decades with the Houston Public Library. (Houston Metropolitan Research Center, Houston Public Library)

Librarian Julia Ideson was a leader in community activities. She was one of the principal initiators of the Houston Open Forum, which from 1926 to 1938 gave Houstonians opportunities to examine controversial issues as it brought distinguished speakers from all over the world. (Houston Metropolitan Research Center, Houston Public Library)

Jimmie May Hicks spent thirty-three years as head librarian of the Heights Branch Library, where she introduced thousands of Houstonians—young and old alike—to the world of books. (Courtesy Barbara Boek)

In 1933 Ruth Wikoff (second from right) was named as Houston Junior College's first professional librarian. She moved with the school when it became the University of Houston and remained on its staff for thirty-four years, serving as a full professor and Associate Director of Libraries. (Special Collections and Archives, University of Houston Libraries)

Settlement houses were established during the Progressive era to provide educational and social programs for immigrants, the working class, and impoverished families. Single college-educated women usually staffed the facilities. In 1916 these women, exemplars of the new field of social work, comprised the staff of Rusk Settlement, one of eight settlement houses ultimately opened in Houston. (Courtesy Bernice Hale)

Corinne Fonde came to Houston in 1916 as the head social worker for Rusk Settlement, the Houston Settlement Association's initial center. Her ardent support of public recreation led in 1918 to the formation of a city Recreation Department, of which Fonde was named director. Fonde Recreation Center in downtown Houston bears her name. (Courtesy San Jacinto Girl Scout Council)

Ellie Walls Montgomery had to leave Texas to obtain a professional education. She was the first black woman in the United States to get a degree in social work. After receiving degrees from Fisk University, Columbia University, and New York School of Philanthropy, she returned to Houston in 1913 and spent the next forty-five years as an educator and social scientist. (Houston Metropolitan Research Center, Houston Public Library)

Heloise Brown Canter passed the Texas CPA examination in May 1942 and became the first female Certified Public Accountant in the Gulf Coast area. During her long career, she was recognized nationally as a leader in the field of accounting. (Houston Metropolitan Research Center, Houston Public Library)

The first professional artists' gallery opened in the basement of the Beaconsfield Apartments on Main Street in 1930. In a true cooperative effort, members scrubbed floors and scavenged for furniture, collected paintings to exhibit, brewed tea for customers, and managed the gallery during business hours. Their efforts enabled artists to gain prestige and credibility within the community. (Courtesy Patricia John Keightley)

CHAPTER VI

Cultivating the Arts

The tenth child of an ex-slave, Naomi Polk grew up in the city's Fourth Ward. Widowed early, she raised three children on $36 a month while rising at 4 a.m. to write, and staying up late into the night to paint on window shades, ceiling tiles, cardboard, and scraps of wood. Polk's unpretentious poetry and expressive paintings reflected her deep religious beliefs and a strong sense of her African-American heritage. During her lifetime Naomi Polk never received recognition for her art; indeed, she never created it for the public eye. She only knew that the need for self-expression was at the core of her being. Not until after her death in 1984 were Polk's works discovered and exhibited.

Houston has produced many women who, like Naomi Polk, have a deep inner desire to give expression to their artistic voices. They have played an active and continuous role in the creation of all types of art whether in the studio, on the stage, or at a desk.

During the nineteenth century, women most often expressed their artistry through china painting and needlework. They hand-painted entire sets of china, most frequently utilizing floral designs but sometimes expanding into landscape scenes. Hand-stitched quilts, crocheted bed spreads, lace tatting, and embroidery were created not only for their practicality but also for the beauty they brought to their surroundings. Such work was considered a lady-like endeavor, and few women in Houston pursued art as anything other than an avocation.

With the establishment of the Museum of Fine Arts in 1924, the city's art consciousness grew, and the need for trained artists was recognized. Some local female artists began teaching classes in their homes, while courses in drawing and painting were offered by the Museum School and the Department of Architecture at Rice Institute. Since women had been involved in promoting art appreciation in the city, it was not surprising that most of the professional artists emerging in the 1920s were females.

For the most part, these women worked individually as they sought to widen their experiences and techniques. They focused primarily on still lifes, portraits, and landscapes. Their subjects were invariably romantic or spiritual in tone, and their work was characterized by displays of vivid color and strong emotion. Eager to join the artistic mainstream, many of these female artists made regular trips to New York, Mexico, Europe, and even north Africa to study and expand their horizons.

At home, however, they had few places to exhibit their art. Although the Museum of Fine Arts sponsored an annual exhibition of local artists' work, and even placed the winning entry in its permanent collection, Houston artists were most often limited to showing their works in private homes, theaters, studios, and paint supply stores. Cognizant that this was an obstacle to the advancement of art, Grace Spaulding John organized Houston's first gallery for professional artists. Not only did the Houston Artists' Gallery sponsor auctions and lectures, but it also became a forum for artistic dialogue. Slowly, an art colony began to form in Houston.

Since Houston was a part of the segregated South, African-American

The Art Club held a dinner in 1908 at which Mrs. Booker T. Washington was the guest speaker. This group promoted cultural activities in a city which was experiencing rapid growth. (Covington Collection, Houston Metropolitan Research Center, Houston Public Library)

In 1931 these women were prominent members of Houston's art colony: (left to right) McNeill Davidson, Virgie Claxton Lowenstein, Grace Spaulding John, Ruth Uhler, Florence Fall, E. Richardson Cherry, Mrs. Robert Buckner Morris, Beatrice Matthei, Mrs. Frederick N. Burton, and Penelope Lingan. (Courtesy Patricia John Keightley)

Sculptor Clare Dieman's artistic expression centered on creating figures which could be used to adorn buildings. In the late 1920s she established a studio in Houston where she produced her works, many representing the frontier spirit of the West. (Courtesy Patricia John Keightley)

artists found few outlets for their work. They primarily supported each other through culture clubs, such as the Ethel Ransom Art and Literary Club. The limited art education available to blacks was sustained through the persistent efforts of women like Willie Lee Thomas, Laura Sands, and Fannie Holman, who taught art in Houston's black schools.

During the Great Depression local artists were hired by the Works Project Administration, a federal agency that employed them to produce works for the interiors of Houston's public buildings. Emma Richardson Cherry, Ruth Uhler, Angela McDonnell, Grace Spaulding John, Virginia Claxton, Stella Shurtleff, and Sarah Kahlder created murals—all historical in nature—for the Houston Public Library, City Hall, and several schools. Cherry later recalled that she probably cleared about eleven cents a day from her work on this project. She and the others had, however, made a significant contribution to public art in Houston.

With the organization of the Contemporary Arts Association in 1948, new attention was focused on modern art. The Association's ideas and exhibitions stimulated the development of artists who broke with traditional forms and moved toward abstract expression. As a result of this growing diversity of expression, Houston became the hub of art activity for the Southwest during the 1950s. Prevalent among locally produced works were the brightly-colored primitive images of Mary Ellen Shipnes and the bold abstracts of Margaret Webb Dreyer. Dorothy Hood, who returned to Houston after working some nineteen years in Latin America, imbued her paintings with intense emotion.

Interest in these local artists was nurtured by a growing number of commercial galleries where works were exhibited and sold. In 1957 Katherine Swenson instituted a new venue by opening a gallery that gave solo shows to local painters. Numerous female art impresarios followed suit by providing gallery space for both traditional and avant-garde works.

Not only did women become dedicated practicioners of artistic

Ruth Uhler (left) and Grace Spaulding John collaborated on a mural for Houston's newly built City Hall in 1939. The mural has been refurbished in a recent renovation of the City Hall foyer. (Courtesy Patricia John Keightley)

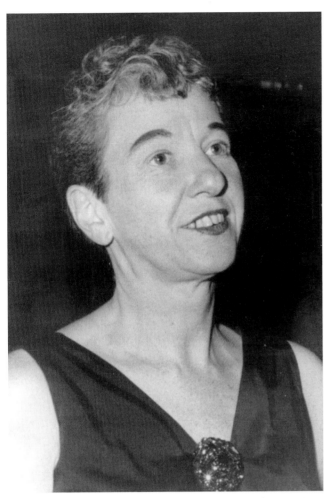

As the first professional director of the Contemporary Arts Museum, Jermayne MacAgy became known for her innovative exhibitions. In 1959 she established an art department at the University of St. Thomas where she lectured extensively and influenced the advancement of contemporary art through her eclectic exhibitions and accompanying catalogues. (Houston Metropolitan Research Center, Houston Public Library)

While Margaret Webb Dreyer was an award-winning artist herself, her impact on the city's art scene went beyond her own work. For fifteen years Dreyer owned and operated a gallery where she exhibited not only recognized artists but also young ones who needed encouragement as well as a place to show their works. (Courtesy Martin Dreyer)

expression but many became enthusiastic patrons of this cultural medium. Perhaps no one was more responsible for promoting art in our city than Dominique de Menil, who insisted that Houston could become a world-class arts center. Her support of art education and exhibitions greatly encouraged aspiring, as well as established, artists.

As literary editor of the *Houston Chronicle* in the 1920s, Katie Daffan was a frequent contributor of literary reviews and essays. She was also a poet of some acclaim.
(Houston Metropolitan Research Center, Houston Public Library)

Houston's art colony continued to grow. Women participated in ever increasing numbers not only as the creators of art, but also as educators, curators, gallery owners, and financial supporters. Their presence is still very much in evidence today.

Literature was another avenue through which women expressed their creativity. An interest in literature had inspired the founding of study clubs in Houston as early as 1885. The Shakespeare Club, Current Literature Club, Houston Heights Literary Club, and Ladies' Reading Club were organized to provide members with opportunities to learn about works of literature. As they read and studied great works from the past, many of these women turned to putting their own thoughts on paper.

Women had long recounted their experiences in diaries and letters. But as early as the 1850s, some women in America had become successful authors, immortalized by Nathaniel Hawthorne's scathing remark about the "damned mob of scribbling women" whose sentimental novels outsold his own. Writing was a natural pursuit for women. It required no formal training and could be done in a woman's home where it was easily combined with her domestic responsibilities. Consequently, many middle-class women wrote, often for pleasure and sometimes for money.

In Houston, women found newspapers to be an available outlet for their short stories, sketches, poems, and letters. Aurelia Hadley Mohl, Claudia Girardeau, Maude Fuller Young, and Willa Lloyd were frequent contributors in the 1880s to local publications like *The Ladies' Messenger*. Because such a pursuit was still considered by many to be less than lady-like, female writers often signed their work with only their first names or perhaps "Anonymous." Many used a pseudonym. Adele Briscoe Looscan, a frequent contributor to *The Ladies' Messenger*, signed her writings "Texan." Women writers also frequently found themselves defending their work to skeptical male editors, who refused to believe that women could write so well.

Among the late nineteenth century writers from our area, the most prolific and certainly the most widely cited in literary circles today is Mollie Evelyn Moore Davis. Although Davis began writing as a teenager, her literary career bloomed when she spent several years living in Houston with a newspaper publisher's family. Her first collection of poetry, *Minding the Gap and Other Poems*, appeared in 1867. By the early 1870s Davis was reaching a national audience. Although she continued to write poetry, she became better known for her short stories, her plays and stories for children, and her book-length prose. In a career spanning almost fifty years, Davis authored twelve books in addition to many articles for literary magazines.

During this time female writers had few opportunities to be part of a network in which they could support one another and further develop their skills. An awareness of this situation led Aurelia Hadley Mohl to organize the Texas Woman's Press Association in 1893. Mohl had established her reputation as a writer in 1865 when Houston's *Tri-Weekly Telegraph* published her short story, "An Afternoon Nap," which predicted a number of later inventions, including the telephone. She had begun her career some ten years earlier when she became head of the literary department of the widely read *Houston Telegraph*. After working in Washington, D.C. as a correspondent for several Texas newspapers, Mohl returned to Houston determined to bring women writers the recognition they deserved. The Texas Woman's Press Association sponsored meetings in which members mapped out plans for entry into the mainstream of literary life.

In 1906 the Houston Pen Women was organized. Its stated purpose was "to encourage young writers and to improve each other's technique and style by holding literary contests." These literary contests became a major feature of the Poetry Society of Texas, which was organized in 1921 and advertised that it was open to any lover of poetry. During the following decade women in Texas started writing poetry seriously, laying the groundwork for one who would become the central figure of female poetry in the region—Vassar Miller.

Miller valiantly pursued her life of creative expression. Hampered physically by cerebral palsy, she nevertheless would rise before dawn to compose her poems, slowly pecking out the words on an electric typewriter. With *Adam's Footprint* in 1956, Miller introduced herself to a national audience. During her career, which spanned four decades, she published ten books of poetry, received a nomination for the Pulitzer Prize in poetry, and won three awards from the Texas Institute of Letters.

The writings of Houston women can be found today on bookshelves, in newspapers and magazines, on film, and in professional journals. Their contributions to the written word have been manifold.

Women played a pivotal role in Houston's musical life as well. In the late nineteenth century, local female musicians exercised their talent mainly in church choirs. Some taught voice and instrumental music in their homes or in the schools. Until music clubs began forming, women had few opportunities to perform in public.

The Philharmonic Society was the first serious music club organized in Houston. Its director was Lucie Palmer Grunewald, a highly trained pianist and longtime teacher of young Houstonians. In 1896 a group of ladies formed a singing society composed entirely of women. Taking the name Treble Clef Club, they regularly presented choral works as community events. Another group, the Thursday Morning Musical Club, which was organized in 1908, required exacting auditions for its members. These pianists, violinists, vocalists, and organists not only presented public concerts but also pursued a rigorous course of study at their meetings.

While clubs brought touring artists of national and international renown to the city, these music lovers ardently wanted their city to have its own musical ensemble. Joining efforts, they persuaded thirty-five local musicians to give a concert on a summer afternoon in 1913. The solo vocalist was a young Houston woman, Blanche Foley, who like many of her contemporaries had studied music in Europe. This single concert gave birth to the Houston Symphony Orchestra, which women have continued to support and encourage through the years.

Scores of young black women built on church and school musical experiences to launch careers singing in gospel choirs, interpreting popular and classical music in concert halls, and performing jazz, rock, or blues.

Invocation

Hurricane, hurricane,
blow me away,
frail as a moth,
light as a leaf;
shake me loose from my skin,
blast me out of my bones,
dancing upon my humanness
grinding it into powder
less than the dust.
Sever me from my heart,
sunder me from my soul
till I am purer than angels,
sinless as God.

　　　　　　　—Vassar Miller

Many of Vassar Miller's poems address religious themes: faith, doubt, suffering, and grace. Most are short, with an intense concentration of thought and emotion.
(*"Invocation" from If I Had Wheels or Love, Collected Poems of Vassar Miller*, reprinted by permission of Southern Methodist University Press)

Women frequently gave voice to their musical talents
by singing in church choirs. Shown here is the
choir of First Presbyterian Church in the 1880s.
(Courtesy First Presbyterian Church)

Trained in piano and voice, Mary
Nicholson McDowell taught music to
young Houstonians for more than sixty
years. (Houston Metropolitan Research
Center, Houston Public Library)

The Houston Heights Music Club became the Music Department of the Houston Heights Woman's Club in 1911. Like its counterparts across the city, the club promoted musical activities for the general population. In the center of the photograph are two charter members of the Heights club: Mrs. D. D. Cooley and Mrs. W. B. Welling. (Houston Metropolitan Research Center, Houston Public Library)

1918   TWENTY-FIFTH SEASON   1919

FIRST CONCERT

Treble Clef Club

MRS. ROBERT L. COX, Conductor
MR. SAM T. SWINFORD, Accompanist

PRESENT

JASCHA HEIFETZ
WORLD-FAMED VIOLINIST

ANDRE BENOIST, ACCOMPANIST

Organized in 1893, the Treble Clef Club had a membership of 672 by 1911. In addition to presenting its own programs, the club began to sponsor visiting artists. In 1919 internationally acclaimed violinist Jascha Heifetz appeared under its auspices. (Elaine Finfrock Roberts Papers, Junior League Component, Houston Metropolitan Research Center, Houston Public Library)

Katherine Putnam Parker, music teacher and Director of the Woman's Choral Club, was a leader in promoting musical activities. She served as the first president of the Houston Symphony Society in 1913, and later was a founding member of the National Symphony Orchestra in Washington, D.C. (Houston Metropolitan Research Center, Houston Public Library)

Many received regional and national acclaim. One woman who learned to perform in church and later caught the "blues bug" was Beulah (Sippie) Wallace, who recorded scores of hits during the 1920s. Jewel Brown debuted as a singer at age nine in a local Masonic temple. After graduating from high school, she embarked on a musical career which reached its zenith as she performed jazz with Louis Armstrong all over the world.

Perhaps no person contributed more to Houston's cultural enrichment than Edna Saunders. A trained musician and an active member of the Woman's Choral Club, Saunders was named booking agent for the City Auditorium in 1910. Over the next half century she became recognized as the most successful impresario in the entire Southwest. Among performers appearing under "Edna Saunders Presents" were Enrico Caruso, Serge Rachmaninoff, Fritz Kreisler, Marian Anderson, John Philip Sousa, Will Rogers, and Katherine Hepburn. In addition, companies such as Ballet Russe de Monte Carlo and the Metropolitan Opera became annual visitors to the city. Houston's present-day Society for the Performing Arts evolved from Saunders' dedication to providing Houstonians with the very finest in cultural experiences.

The public's growing interest in opera and ballet resulted in the formation of two resident companies in 1955. Civic leader Elva Lobit brought together a group of opera lovers who chose two works to be presented, adopted a budget, and named a general director. Houston Grand Opera was born that night in Mrs. Lobit's living room.

Similarly, a group of local balletomanes met to form a permanent dance company. Under the guidance of former Ballet Russe de Monte Carlo dancers Tatiana Semenova and Nina Popova, the company opened a training academy and began to give public performances. Houston Ballet, along with the Houston Symphony Orchestra and Houston Grand Opera, enabled the city to become one of America's premier centers for the performing arts. Women continued to be actively involved in this process, as both performers and patrons.

Dramatic arts were popular in Houston from its earliest days. Theaters flourished as traveling troupes presented plays which ranged from *My Sister Dear* to *Hamlet*. By the late nineteenth century local groups, using homes and gardens of members, were staging productions to entertain the city's residents and at the same time to provide opportunities for aspiring local actors. The Shakespeare Club presented *As You Like It* on the tree-shaded lawn of the Emanuel Raphael home while numerous events were held at the home of Mrs. Robert Duff, a musician and patron of the arts. These offerings sometimes met with opposition. In an effort to raise funds for a new building, members of the Ladies' Parish Association of Christ Church presented *H.M.S. Pinafore* at Gray's Opera House despite strenuous objections from their priest.

Not until the Little Theatre movement began sweeping across the country after World War I, however, was there a concentrated effort to establish a permanent venue for the dramatic arts. Groups like the Red Lantern Players and the Green Mask Players were short-lived. Then on September 25, 1925, the Houston Little Theatre was organized to provide "the opportunity of self expression in the art of acting, and to present to the people of Houston the opportunity of seeing productions which have as their ideal the promotion of high-class pleasurable drama."

Women filled many roles in the Houston Little Theatre. They served as board members, fund raisers, actresses, publicists, and patrons. Mary E. Ben Isaacs played a particularly important role in the Houston Negro Little Theatre. Isaacs, a playwright and teacher, directed this group during the years of the Great Depression and enabled it to survive those hard economic times.

In 1947 a young drama teacher named Nina Vance sent 214 penny postcards to persons she thought might be interested in paying a dime to become members of a new theater group. The response was so favorable that production began immediately on *A Sound of Hunting*, which was presented in a cramped dance studio off a Main Street alleyway. That was the beginning of the Alley Theatre, the first resident professional theater of its kind outside of New York. The success of the Alley led to the formation of other theaters in the city—the Playhouse, Kuumba House, Main Street Theater, Stages, A. D. Players. As theater has expanded in Houston, women have been leaders in all aspects of its operation—as actresses, directors, producers, stagehands, publicists, fund raisers, and audience.

Women have long been considered the bearers of culture within a community. Certainly in Houston they have borne that role as creators, performers, patrons, and promoters of the arts. As a result, the city has benefited in extraordinary ways from these women whose efforts have brought such rich cultural experiences into our midst.

Ima Hogg, pictured here with conductor Sir John Barbarolli, was at the heart of the Houston Symphony Orchestra's operations throughout her long life. Serving as president of the Houston Symphony Society for fourteen years, she remained a committed supporter in every aspect of the orchestra's existence. (Courtesy Houston Symphony Society)

Dedicated teachers trained young musicians in every avenue of musical performance. These harpists, performing at the Rice Institute May Fete in 1933, were students of Mildred Milligan, who taught countless Houstonians during her long career. (Courtesy Patricia John Keightley)

Opposite page top: The Woman's Committee of the Houston Symphony Society was organized in 1937 to assist in raising funds. When this photograph was made in 1946, the committee had just completed a successful subscription campaign. Over the years, its duties expanded to sponsoring educational programs and promoting the orchestra. It has even added to the orchestra's repertoire by commissioning new works. (Houston Metropolitan Research Center, Houston Public Library)

Opposite page bottom: The Ladies' Symphony Orchestra was organized in 1915 by Jennie Belle Covington. Conducted by Madame Corilla Rochon, the ensemble frequently performed in the community. (Covington Collection, Houston Metropolitan Research Center, Houston Public Library)

Opposite page: After receiving her earliest instruction in Houston, Patricia John became an internationally acclaimed harpist. Throughout her career she concertized, taught, and composed. Her compositions for the harp can be found in collections worldwide. (Courtesy Patricia John Keightley)

Artist unknown, *Chocolate Set*, circa. 1900, Hand-painted china. (Courtesy Billy K. Chapman)

Sue Dee Grainger Brown, *Crazy Quilt*, circa 1886. (From *Lone Stars: A Legacy of Texas Quilts, 1836–1936* by Karoline Patterson Bresenhan and Nancy O'Bryant Puentes, copyright 1986. Courtesy of the authors and the University of Texas Press)

E. Richardson Cherry, *Precious Bowl*, circa. 1925, oil on canvas.

(Courtesy The Museum of Fine Arts, Houston; gift of Mrs. William Chilton Maverick)

Grace Spaulding John, *Easter*, 1933, oil on canvas. (Courtesy Patricia John Keightley)

Ruth Pershing Ulher, *Untitled (Fantastic Landscape)*, 1930, oil on canvas. (Courtesy The Museum of Fine Arts, Houston; gift of Alice C. Simkins)

Mabel Fairfax Karl, *Orpheus and Eurydice*, circa. 1934, wood. (Courtesy The Museum of Fine Arts, Houston; 10th Annual Houston Artists Exhibition Museum Prize, 1934)

Angela McDonnell, *Avila*, 1934, mural
in Julia Ideson Building, Houston Public
Library. (Courtesy Houston Public Library)

Greco-Roman, *Myrtle Wreath*, 330–250
B.C., gold. (Courtesy The Museum of Fine
Arts, Houston; gift of Miss Annette Finnigan)

Cross Vine

Eloise Reid Thompson 38

Eloise Reid Thompson, *Cross Vine*, **n.d., watercolor.** (Courtesy Museum of Natural Science, Houston)

Dorothy Hood, *Haiti,* 1969, oil on canvas.
(Courtesy The Museum of Fine Arts, Houston; gift of Mr. and Mrs. Meredith Long)

Clare Dieman, *Pojoaque,* 1959, wood.
(Courtesy John Spaulding John)

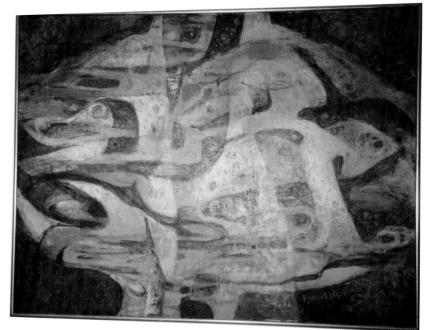

Margaret Webb Dreyer, *Sequence*, 1974, acrylic. (Courtesy Martin Dreyer)

Ruth London, *East Terrace Garden, Bayou Bend*, landscape design, 1936. (Courtesy The Museum of Fine Arts, Houston; The Bayou Bend Collection and Gardens; photo by Rick Gardner)

The Ballroom, *Rienzi.* (Courtesy The Museum of Fine Arts, Houston; photo by Paul Hester)

(Legend for painting on pages 138-139) **This painting by Carole Bunge Halla is symbolic of Houston's growth from a primitive settlement on the bayou to the nation's fourth largest city. In it we see** images of Houston's past and present—an early paddle wheeler on Buffalo Bayou, the Museum of Fine Arts, the 1904 Market House, Methodist Hospital, City Hall, and the city's skyline in the year 2000. Almost invisible in the painting, but definitely a part of it, are women representing a broad spectrum of time and backgrounds. Looking closely, we can see a young woman of the early nineteenth century, who may only have dreamed of settling in Texas; an African-American female in modern native dress; a woman of the present, looking to the future; a Native American woman, one of the original inhabitants of the area; a mature pioneer woman when Houston was on the frontier; and in the center a young woman of the early twentieth century, an era when women came from their parlors into the public sphere and when Houston became important as a major American city. Women have been integral threads in the Houston tapestry for more than 160 years. As our city enters the twenty-first century, it will, undoubtedly, continue to be strengthened and enriched by the presence of women.

Mary Ellen Shipnes, *Kristi's Garden*, 1985, oil on board.
(Courtesy Mary Ellen Shipnes, photographed by Sarah Hazelgrove)

Gutzon Borglum, *Peggy*, 1927, bronze and granite. This sculpture, one of the few in our city honoring a woman, is named for Elizabeth (Peggy) McGregor. It is located in McGregor Park. (Photo by author)

Lone Star Chapter of the American Needlepoint Guild, *Houston Past and Present*, 1986, needle-point. This 8'x 8' artwork, a gift to the city in commemoration of its sesquicentennial celebration, hangs in the Julia Ideson Building of the Houston Public Library. (Courtesy Houston Public Library)

Lauren Anderson as Aurora in Houston Ballet's production of *Sleeping Beauty.* (Courtesy Houston Ballet; photo by Drew Donovan)

Little Women, **Houston Grand Opera production featuring Jennifer Aylmer as Amy, Laura A. Coker as Beth, Stephanie Novacek as Jo, and Joyce DiDonato as Meg.** (Courtesy Houston Grand Opera; photo by Jim Caldwell)

Lydia Mendoza began her career performing with her family in their East End neighborhood. The Mendozas' subsequent tours in the 1930s catapulted Lydia to international fame. Her melodious voice and skill on the twelve-string guitar earned her the title "Meadowlark of the Border," and resulted in hundreds of recordings being made. (Houston Metropolitan Research Center, Houston Public Library)

This theatrical group in Magnolia Park was indicative of the growing Mexican population in Houston during the 1920s. Their performances were popular at community gatherings in the Second Ward neighborhood. (Houston Metropolitan Research Center, Houston Public Library)

Mrs. John Wesley Graham, or "Ma" as she was affectionately known, pioneered the first music concert over local radio in 1922 and continued to broadcast weekly student concerts. After organizing the Civic Opera Company, she presented a lavish production of *Aida*, which was repeated at the World's Fair in Chicago in August 1933. She is shown here (second from left) with members of the St. Louis Municipal Opera, one of whom had been her voice student. (Houston Metropolitan Research Center, Houston Public Library)

Jazz singer and dancer Daisy Richards (seen on the left) launched her stage career at the Majestic Theater at age fifteen. In 1939 a tour of neighboring states catapulted her to an illustrious career in which she teamed with such performers as Billie Holliday, Count Basie, Lena Horne, and Ella Fitzgerald. (Texas Jazz Archives, Houston Metropolitan Research Center, Houston Public Library, courtesy Jazz Heritage Society of Texas)

Ventura Alonzo and her accordion popularized the South Texas *ranchera* style of music in Houston. Alonzo was not only the accordionist and vocalist for the musical group *Alonzo y Sus Rancheros*, but she was also a composer. (Frank and Ventura Alonzo Collection, Houston Metropolitan Research Center, Houston Public Library)

In spite of her father's admonition that being booking agent for a public auditorium was no job for a lady, Edna Saunders persisted and became one of the most successful impresarios in the Southwest. During her fifty-year career, she was a strong force in shaping the culture of Houstonians through entertainment and education. (Houston Metropolitan Research Center, Houston Public Library)

Lillian Culmore, who had studied at the Academy of Dramatic Arts in New York, taught drama and staged extravagant historical pageants for Houston audiences. In 1919 she was a founder of the city's first Little Theatre, which, although shortlived, nevertheless paved the way for subsequent successful efforts in establishing theatrical venues. (Houston Metropolitan Research Center, Houston Public Library)

As a child Dewey Roussel wanted to wear red tights and to ride a horse bareback in the circus. Instead, she gravitated to drama as one of the organizers, and later president, of the Houston Little Theatre. In the 1940s she also filled many acting roles. Roussel (second from right), portrayed Marmee in *Little Women.* (Courtesy Roussel Family Collection)

Margo Jones came to Houston as a young woman in 1936 to head the Federal Theatre Project, an arm of the government's WPA program. When the project folded, Jones formed the Houston Community Players. An innovative director, she staged Houston's first theater-in-the-round productions and dreamed of establishing a resident professional theater. World War II interrupted her plans, but Margo Jones had planted the seeds for future repertory groups that would be daring, permanent, and professional. (Houston Metropolitan Research Center, Houston Public Library)

Johnny George (left), began her career as a director with the Alley Theatre. Later, in 1953, she and two partners formed Theatre, Inc. to present musicals. Under George, Theatre, Inc. remained popular among Houston's theater-goers until it closed in 1966. (*Houston Chronicle*)

As director of the Alley Theatre for thirty-three years, Nina Vance was a trailblazer in theatrical development. She consistently chose plays of high literary quality with morally provocative themes. Many of these were presented at the Alley in premiere performances. (Houston Metropolitan Research Center, Houston Public Library)

Nina Cullinan's philanthropy extended into many sectors of the city's life: arts, mental health, and park land. At her death, she willed more than half of her estate for the development of new parks. Cullinan frequently made anonymous donations and placed few restrictions on charitable gifts. (Houston Metropolitan Research Center, Houston Public Library)

CHAPTER VII

Enriching the Community

It became obvious in 1912 that Faith Home, a community-supported institution for dependent children, needed larger quarters in order to adequately care for its young charges. Operating a facility of this magnitude had, however, drained its coffers, and it appeared that funding a new facility would be difficult. At that point, Faith Home Board member Harriet Levy stepped forward and donated land for a new building. Just as women had been instrumental in founding this much-needed institution, so they continued to be generous with both their time and financial resources, as reflected by Miss Levy's gift.

Over the years Houston's female population has recognized needs in the community and has provided the means to meet those needs. The arts, education, healthcare, and social services have benefited greatly from the generosity of such women as Ima Hogg, Nina Cullinan, Sarah Campbell Blaffer, Carroll Sterling Masterson, Anna Dupree, Annette Finnigan, Ella Cochrum Fondren, Dominique de Menil, Alice Pratt Brown, Audrey Jones Beck, and Caroline Weiss Law. These names are found in public places as a permanent reminder of the philanthropy of these women.

Other lesser-known women have also enriched life in our city. During Houston's early years, women made their greatest contributions through fund-raising campaigns rather than individual gifts. These efforts usually drew upon domestic skills as women busily painted, baked, knitted, and sewed the articles to be sold at charity fairs and bazaars. Community institutions became increasingly dependent on women's fundraising abilities.

The importance of such work has continued through the years with scores of women giving countless hours of their time and utilizing their many talents in supporting a myriad of community activities. Most of these women have never received individual recognition, but their phil-

An avid collector, Sarah Campbell Blaffer wanted to share her interest in art with others. After her death in 1977, the foundation that she had formed created several collections containing Blaffer's own pieces. These collections are exhibited free of charge in small towns around Texas for the enjoyment and enlightenment of those who might otherwise never have such an experience. (Courtesy Sarah Campbell Blaffer Foundation, Houston)

anthropic efforts nevertheless have made a profound difference in our city.

Through gifts of time and money, women—whether individually or as part of a group—have built institutions, funded charitable services, introduced reforms, and addressed inequities in the community. Their generosity has greatly enriched our city.

Health, education, and religion were major concerns of Ella Cochrum Fondren. The Methodist Hospital, Rice University, and United Methodist institutions benefited greatly from Mrs. Fondren's generosity. Her personal credo was: "No individual is honored as an individual. His life takes on dignity as the cause to which he attaches himself takes on dignity." (Courtesy The Methodist Hospital)

Annette Finnigan expressed a strong attachment to her hometown through her gifts. She helped the Museum of Fine Arts build its first permanent collections during the 1930s, and an endowment left to the Houston Public Library upon her death provides the library annually with rare research materials. Finnigan Park furnished a much-needed recreational area in the Fifth Ward when it was given to the city in 1939. (Houston Metropolitan Research Center, Houston Public Library)

Dominique de Menil championed artistic and humanitarian causes throughout her life. Her legacy to the community lies in the Menil Collection and the Byzantine Fresco Chapel Museum, which house priceless pieces of art for public viewing; the Rothko Chapel, an ecumenical place of meditation; and the Carter-Menil Human Rights Award, given biennially to honor human rights activists. (Courtesy Menil Collection; photo by Mike Stude)

Audrey Jones Beck began collecting art as a young woman. Over the next fifty years, she acquired an extraordinary collection while quietly supporting the Museum of Fine Arts. When the collection was given to the museum, the building housing it was named the Audrey Jones Beck Building. Its opening in March 2000 marked a new era for the museum. (Courtesy Museum of Fine Arts, Houston; photo by Richard Barnes)

The imprint of the Brown Foundation, established by the George and Herman Brown families in 1951, can be found all across the city, especially in higher education and the arts. Alice Pratt Brown played a prominent role in these philanthropies while serving for twenty-six years as a trustee of the Museum of Fine Arts. (Archives, Museum of Fine Arts, Houston)

In 1940 Edith Hudson Ripley built a community center on the east side of Houston as a memorial to her husband. Ripley House—the largest such complex in the city at that time—provided a wide variety of services through its gymnasium, auditorium, branch library, nursery school, woodworking and sewing classes, and medical facilities. Ripley House still serves the community today. (Photo by author)

Carroll Sterling Masterson (left), shown here on the lawn of her home, was a benefactor of local medical institutions, as well as cultural organizations. Her most visible gift to Houstonians was Rienzi, the home which she and her husband filled with priceless art and antiques. Rienzi, a decorative arts wing of the Museum of Fine Arts, Houston, attracts many visitors throughout the year. (Houston Metropolitan Research Center, Houston Public Library)

Anna Dupree (second from left), generously funded a home for dependent children, as well as a home for the aged. She also provided funds for the first building at Texas State College for Negroes—now Texas Southern University—and helped to finance the first Little League for black children in Houston. The Anna Dupree Terrace for Senior Citizens was named for her in 1981. (Anna Dupree Collection, Houston Metropolitan Research Center, Houston Public Library)

Ima Hogg has often been called "First Lady of Houston" for her multi-faceted contributions to the city. She was a founder and lifelong supporter of the Houston Symphony Orchestra. Her involvement with the Museum of Fine Arts resulted in the gift of her home, Bayou Bend, and its extraordinary furnishings to the museum. Her interest in mental health led to the establishment of the Houston Child Guidance Center and the Hogg Foundation for Mental Health at the University of Texas. (Archives, Museum of Fine Arts, Houston)

A group of Texas women, led by three dressed in white, marched in a suffrage parade under the Texas banner in Washington, D.C., on April 7, 1913. Suffragists discovered that parades were an effective tool in promoting their cause.

(Reprinted by permission of Ruthe Winegarten and Judith N. McArthur, ed., *Citizens at Last, the Woman Suffrage Movement in Texas*, pg.28)

CHAPTER VIII

Opening New Doors

The *Houston Post* reported on February 17, 1891: "Mrs. Corra B. Foster, energetic well-known real estate dealer . . . property owner and tax payer . . . appeared at the 3rd Ward polls and voted on the bond amendment. Mrs. Foster has thus given evidence of her interest in the city's welfare and expressed herself in the most emphatic manner." The article did not reveal whether the insistent Mrs. Foster's vote was actually counted. After all, women at that time were not part of the electorate. It would be another twenty-nine years before the Constitution of the United States gave females a voice at the ballot box.

In defining qualified electors, the 1876 Constitution of Texas named only "male persons." Women felt that this, by implication, put them in a class with "idiots, lunatics, paupers, and felons," who were specifically disenfranchised. When Texas became a state in 1845, not only were women unable to vote, but also other rights, especially those of married women, were greatly curtailed. A woman's husband controlled all community property acquired during the marriage, including the wife's wages if she worked, as well as any property she inherited or acquired separately. In divorce proceedings, husbands nearly always gained custody of the children. Moreover, married women could not enter into contractual agreements and were, therefore, legally prevented from engaging in business of any kind.

While single women were not faced with these inequities, they had no voice in how their tax dollars were used, since they could not vote. Women became increasingly aware that without the vote they could have little impact on reforming society. They were weary of conducting endless, and often futile, petition drives and lobbying campaigns to persuade legislators and civic leaders to enact needed reforms. Thus began a long and difficult journey in which women struggled to become participants in the political process.

Women traveled about the state gathering support for their suffrage battle. As they traveled from town to town, the suffragists held mass meetings, circulated petitions, sponsored public lectures, and delivered talks before clubs and other groups. At one point, approximately fifteen hundred women were on the speaking circuit in Texas. (Minnie Fisher Cunningham Collection, Houston Metropolitan Research Center, Houston Public Library)

In 1848 the first women's rights convention in the United States was held at Seneca Falls, New York. Thus began a movement that challenged the unequal social and political position of American women and worked to gain more political power for them. Although the national movement continued its attempt to secure suffrage for women, there was little such activity in Texas. Efforts in the mid-1890s were of short duration and produced no lasting results in the state.

The revival of the Texas movement took place in Houston in February 1903 in the home of Katherine, Annette, and Elizabeth Finnigan where thirty-five enthusiastic women formed the Houston Equal Suffrage League. Within a few months the local group organized a state association, electing Annette Finnigan president. It met with only limited success and completely dissolved when the Finnigan family moved from the city.

Upon her return to Houston in 1909, Annette Finnigan renewed her crusade for woman suffrage. She organized the Woman's Political Union, which grew rapidly as more women began to take an interest in expanding their political rights. The state organization was also revived, and once again Finnigan was elected president. Setting up state headquarters in Houston's Brazos Hotel, she initiated a campaign to persuade state legislators to submit a constitutional amendment on suffrage to the Texas electorate. Her letters to them insisted that "it is manifestly unfair and un-

American that the political liberties of half of our citizens should be denied by the will of an indifferent or adverse Legislature." While Finnigan received some supportive replies, most were negative ones such as "Politicks (sic) are too bad for a lady to mix in" and "I do not believe that God intended for woman to have the control of man." Undaunted, in 1915 the persistent Finnigan spent several months in Austin lobbying members of the legislature. Although the proposed amendment failed, the issue of extending the vote to women was now very much before the public.

The suffrage campaign continued with new momentum. Other women with leadership roles in the local movement were Hortense Ward, an attorney who wrote fiery editorials on behalf of the vote and used her political skills as a lobbyist in Austin; Julia Ideson, a librarian who supported professional opportunities for women; Julia Runge, a social reformer who believed that voting rights would be the first step to equalizing salaries between men and women; and Eva Goldsmith, a seamstress and union activist who was concerned with improving working conditions for women.

As the campaign progressed, it drew participation from members of such groups as the City Federation of Women's Clubs, the Housewives League, the Woman's Christian Temperance Union, the YWCA, and Mothers' Clubs. These women joined together in sponsoring suffrage schools, open-air rallies, and massive fundraising meetings. At the same time, suffragists worked hard in supporting the country's efforts in World War I—selling war bonds, planting vegetable gardens, promoting food conservation, rolling bandages, and volunteering for war relief agencies.

Finally their efforts paid off. In March 1918 Governor W. P. Hobby signed a measure giving Texas women the right to vote in a primary election. Three months later 14,750 Harris County women registered for the first time. Victory was complete on August 26, 1920. On that date the Nineteenth Amendment to the United States Constitution was adopted. Using the words of suffragist Susan B. Anthony when she first proposed a

Who Represents Her?

IF a woman is responsible for an accident, if she defaults on her contracts, if she slanders her neighbors, is any man arrested, sued, bound over to keep the peace?

IF a woman steals from her employer, does her father, husband, brother or son serve out her term in prison?

IF a woman kills somebody, what man represents her in the prisoner's dock during her trial? What man represents her in the electric chair if she is convicted?

IF a widow or an unmarried woman fails to pay her taxes, is the property of a male relative or of the man next door sold to satisfy the debt to the State?

IF a woman forges a check, does her father, her husband, her employer, go to jail for felony?

WHY is it that the only place in the world where man wants to represent woman is at the ballot box?

? ? ?

Vote and work for the Suffrage Amendment May 24

TEXAS EQUAL SUFFRAGE ASSOCIATION

BALDWINS———AUSTIN

Suffragists across the state were vigilant in keeping the public informed about their ongoing campaign to receive voting rights. Broadsides like this one were widely distributed. (Minnie Fisher Cunningham Collection, Houston Metropolitan Research Center, Houston Public Library)

woman suffrage amendment in 1878, it read: "The rights of citizens of the United States to vote shall not be denied or abridged by the United States or by any State on account of sex." It had been seventy-two years, one month and one week since that meeting in Seneca Falls when women had first convened to demand their "sacred right" to vote.

Women who had worked so long for their voting rights wanted an organization to help all women exercise their political rights. On August 18, 1920, one week before the ratification of the Nineteenth Amendment, a group met over luncheon at the Rice Hotel and officially organized the League of Women Voters of Houston. Their first act was to hire a brass band to lead a jubilee march down Main Street. Their second and more important task was to develop a program to encourage informed voting by both women and men. They began by providing factual non-partisan information through league-sponsored forums and candidate rallies. Topics included government structure, participation in political activities, education and school funding, improvement of city services, and addressing the needs of women and children.

As women were being praised for their patriotic activities during World War I, they reminded the public that patriotism and responsibility were inseparable and that they wanted the responsibility associated with voting. A local newspaper in 1916 published this drawing which set forth Suffrage, Preparedness, and Americanism as ideal achievements of womanhood. (Houston Metropolitan Research Center, Houston Public Library)

The local league joined with others across the nation to ensure passage of the Sheppard-Towner Act for the welfare of mothers and infants; the Cable Act for independent citizenship of married women; the Civil Service Reclassification Act, which provided equal compensation for women; the Tennessee Valley Authority Act for conservation and responsible development of natural resources; the Social Security Act, which provided federally-administered old-age insurance; and the Food, Drug and Cosmetic Act, which required that such items meet specific quality standards. All of these issues were of great concern to women as were laws that regulated child labor. Women came to the full realization that their ability to vote and to participate in the political process enabled them to influence public policy and to work toward improving life not only for women but also for the entire populace.

Although women had gained a voice at the polls, their entry into the political arena as elected officials was a slow one. Education reformers had long argued that women, as experts on child development, should serve on school boards. The Houston Equal Suffrage League tried as early as 1904 to have women named to the board of the Houston City Schools, but they were unsuccessful. In 1917, however, Mrs. Charles Scholibo was appointed to the board. Then, over the next four years, several more women were named. When these positions became elective ones in 1923, Mrs. D. D. Cooley, Mrs. Maurice Goldman, and Mrs. W. B. Morrison were elected to the Board of Education for the newly formed Houston Independent School District. Women have served on school boards throughout the Houston area in every decade since.

Serving on school boards, however, did not lead to other offices. In the first years after winning the suffrage battle, few women ran for public office. A rare exception occurred in 1920 when three women were candidates on the ticket of the Black and Tan wing of the Republican party. Mrs. G. B. M. Turner ran for county school superintendent, Mrs. R. L. Yocome filed for state representative, and Mrs. F. L. Long was on the ballot for county clerk. Although all lost, their actions confirmed that women could run for public office and attract voters.

Women's support of the war effort helped swing public sentiment in favor of suffrage. Their activities on the home front were vital to achieving victory. (Houston Metropolitan Research Center, Houston Public Library)

During World War I a group of coeds at Rice Institute formed the Women's Army Corps. While they were not an official military unit, they showed that women could be an important factor in building support for worthy causes. (Woodson Research Center, Fondren Library, Rice University)

Soon after the 1920 election, black women found themselves involved in a major political issue. The 1923 passage of a law prohibiting blacks from voting in a Democratic party primary essentially prevented them from participating in the electoral process since Texas was basically a one-party state at that time. At this point, many black Houstonians became involved in another struggle—acquiring the same civil rights accorded white citizens. This was the beginning of a new movement in which women would play key roles over the next four decades.

Through their involvement with such organizations as the National Association for the Advancement of Colored People and Black Women for Social Change, disenfranchised women worked for an end to the white primary and against the crime of lynching. They also reached across racial lines to unite with white women in attempting to end discrimination. The Committee on Women's Work of the Texas Commission on Interracial Cooperation worked to implement such things in Houston as placing paved streets in black neighborhoods, establishing an employment bureau for young women, sponsoring courses in race relations, and founding one of the first black Girl Scout troops in the South.

Mexican American women became more active in the political process during the 1960s through their involvement with groups such as the Political Association of Spanish Speaking Organizations, The League of United Latin American Citizens, and La Raza Unida. Their visibility increased as they worked in political campaigns and eventually ran for public office.

In spite of increased political activity, women continued to have little success in being elected to public office. In the post-suffrage decades, only a few Texas women were elected to positions in state government. The state's two major political parties resisted attempts to place women on state and county executive committees, thus negating the representation of women in the political process. Not until 1973 did Harris County elect its first female members of the Texas House of Representatives—Kay Bailey and Senfronia Thompson.

Harris County had sent its first woman to the Texas Senate in 1947 when Maribelle Stewart was elected to fill the seat left vacant after her husband died. In 1966 attorney Barbara Jordan won a seat in that body as the first black since Reconstruction. In 1972 Jordan again was a trailblazer as the first black woman elected to Congress from the South, representing the 18th Congressional District. During her six-year tenure in the United

States House of Representatives, she became an eloquent voice for the democratic principles that she so vehemently supported. Jordan's election also paved the way for other women who successfully gained public office in the years following.

In 1974 Congresswoman Jordan appeared before the House Judiciary Committee. In her presentation, she declared: "Earlier today, we heard the beginning of the Preamble to the Constitution of the United States. We the people. It is a very eloquent beginning. But when that document was completed on the 17th of September in 1787, I was not included in that We the people . . . But, through the process of amendment, interpretation and court decision, I have finally been included in We the people."

Like Barbara Jordan, most women—regardless of their ethnic background or their economic status—can today claim full citizenship. As women exercise their rights in the voting booth, or participate at the grassroots level of a political campaign, or run for elective office, they are making a profound difference in our society. Their voices give expression to what is, their vision illuminates what can be, and their willingness to work for change creates a better community. As doors have opened to women, affording them new opportunities, so they continue to open doors to those who follow.

Louise Masterson played an important role in the local suffrage campaign, serving as an officer of both the Woman's Political Union and its successor, the Harris County Equal Suffrage Association. Masterson continued her political activism in the League of Women Voters, which she served as its third president.
(Houston Metropolitan Research Center, Houston Public Library)

As president of the City Federation of Women's Clubs in 1918, Elizabeth Ring was a strong voice for woman suffrage. She also lobbied for protective legislation for women and children in industry and a minimum wage law for working women. Ring's campaign for prison reform in the 1920s resulted in significant changes in the Texas penal system.
(Houston Metropolitan Research Center, Houston Public Library)

Business executive Florence Sterling expanded her suffrage involvement into becoming a founder of the Houston branch of the League of Women Voters. She later became the first executive secretary of the League's national organization. (Houston Metropolitan Research Center, Houston Public Library)

In 1922 the League of Women Voters held a state convention in Houston. The city rolled out the welcome mat for delegates. This cartoon, alluding to the idea that women had a cleansing effect on politics through their actions at the polls, appeared in a local newspaper following the meeting. (League of Women Voters Collection, Houston Metropolitan Research Center, Houston Public Library)

As a proponent of women's rights, Hortense Ward worked to get the Married Woman's Property Law of 1913 passed by the Texas Legislature. She also campaigned for a fifty-four-hour week for women in industry, a domestic relations court, and the right of women to serve as officers of corporations. Ward continued throughout her life to be a strong voice on issues relevant to women's lives.

(Archives Department, Gov. Bill and Vara Daniel Center for Legal History, Austin)

In Two Parts

Part One

THE WOMAN'S VIEWPOINT

NOVEMBER · 1925   PRICE 15 CENTS   VOL. III · No. 7

A MAGAZINE SERVING HUMANITY

EDITED AND PUBLISHED BY WOMEN

The Woman's Viewpoint, a magazine produced by an all-female editorial staff headed by Florence Sterling, publicized women's achievements and stressed their obligation to participate in civic and political affairs. During its existence from 1923 to 1927, the publication advocated clean government, strong prohibition and drug enforcement laws, and world peace. (Houston Metropolitan Research Center, Houston Public Library)

Re-elect
DR. RAY K. DAILY
to
SCHOOL BOARD POSITION 4
Houston Independent School District
(Election Tuesday, Nov. 4, 1952)

*Houston Needs Sound Experience
in This Time of Educational Crisis*

26

Look at her record and platform (over)

Women actively campaigned for positions on school boards, and after election frequently served long tenures. Ray Daily, a twenty-five-year member of the board of the Houston Independent School District, served as its first female president as well as president of the State Association of School Boards. (Ray K. Daily Collection, Houston Metropolitan Research Center, Houston Public Library)

The Houston Independent School District Board of Trustees often found itself divided on issues. During the 1950s and 1960s, battles were fought over desegregating schools, accepting federal funds, and requiring non-communist loyalty oaths. The female members in this 1956 photograph are Verna Rogers (president), **Mary Porter Vandervoort**, and **Dallas Dyer**. (Houston Metropolitan Research Center, Houston Public Library)

Most meetings of the HISD board were packed with women during the 1950s. These years of turbulence, fostered by conflicting attitudes of progressivism and conservatism, created extreme unrest in the school system. Women, having discovered their political voices, could be found on both sides of most issues. As a result, the exchanges were often heated. (Houston Metropolitan Research Center, Houston Public Library)

When she was elected to the board of the Houston Independent School District in 1958, Hattie Mae White became the first black Texan elected to public office since Reconstruction. She served as a member for nine years. Today the district's administration building is named for White. (UT Institute of Texan Cultures at San Antonio, courtesy Stan Begam)

Jennie Belle Covington, who had been a founder of the Blue Triangle branch of the YWCA in Houston, became chairman of the Negro Women's Division of the Texas Commission on Inter-racial Cooperation in 1926. In this capacity she traveled around the state speaking before groups and raising funds for its work. (Covington Collection, Houston Metropolitan Research Center, Houston Public Library)

Lulu B. White, executive secretary of the Houston branch of the NAACP, was known as "matriarch of the civil rights movement in Texas" for her leadership from 1939 to 1949. (Houston Metropolitan Research Center, Houston Public Library)

Christia Adair began her career as a political activist by campaigning for women's voting rights. When she was denied the right to vote in the 1918 Texas primary election because she was black, she became active in the civil rights movement. One of Houston's first black precinct judges, Adair was a respected leader for over fifty years. A Harris County park was named for her in 1994. (Christia Adair Collection, Houston Metropolitan Research Center, Houston Public Library)

Frankie Carter Randolph was a powerful participant in Texas politics. Working as a volunteer at every level, she championed racial equality and social justice. In 1956 Randolph was elected Democratic National Committeewoman from Texas. She was also a founder of the *Texas Observer* newspaper. (Courtesy *Texas Observer*)

In 1935 the first Ladies' LULAC Council was formed. By the late 1940s Ladies LULAC Council #22, pictured here, had been organized and was addressing such issues as discrimination in housing, education, and employment. These women soon realized that their voices made a difference in the public arena. (Houston Metropolitan Research Center, Houston Public Library)

Over the past eighty years, the non-partisan League of Women Voters has worked to develop an informed electorate. Information on the functions of government and the responsibilities of citizenship has been disseminated through league representatives, pictured here in 1955, and its pre-election Voters' Guide, which has been distributed since the 1960s. (League of Women Voters Collection, Houston Metropolitan Research Center, Houston Public Library)

Women were prohibited from serving on Texas juries until 1954. In June 1959 an all-female jury was selected for the first time to hear a case in Harris County civil courts. (Houston Metropolitan Research Center, Houston Public Library)

In 1953 Oveta Culp Hobby was appointed by President Dwight Eisenhower as the first Secretary of Health, Education and Welfare. Her prior experience in government affairs provided her with valuable insights as she organized this new department of the federal government. Upon her return to Houston in 1955, Hobby resumed her position as president and editor of the *Houston Post.* Her influence in the community continued through her journalistic voice and her participation in civic affairs. (Houston Metropolitan Research Center, Houston Public Library)

During her second term in the Texas Senate, Barbara Jordan was named "governor for a day." She thus became the first black woman to serve as a state's chief executive. In 1994 Jordan was awarded the Presidential Medal of Freedom, the nation's highest civilian honor, for her work in civil rights. (Texas State Library & Archives Commission)

In 1977 Kathy Whitmire became the first female ever elected to a city-wide office in Houston. After serving as Controller for two terms, Whitmire became the first woman to occupy the mayoral chair—a position she held for ten years. (Courtesy Kathy Whitmire; photo by Kaye Marvins)

In 1979 Eleanor Tinsley, whose political career had begun ten years earlier when she won a seat on the HISD Board, was elected to the Houston City Council. During her sixteen years on the council Tinsley was a strong advocate for neighborhood parks, historic preservation, building and transportation safety, and sign control. (*Houston Chronicle*)

Christin Hartung was elected to Houston City Council in 1979, giving her the distinction, along with Eleanor Tinsley, of being one of two women first elected to this position. Hartung worked on the council to improve the quality of life for citizens by focusing on law enforcement, fire safety, and emergency medical services. (*Houston Chronicle*)

As a news reporter covering sessions of the Texas legislature for a Houston television station, Kay Bailey decided that Texas needed a stronger two-party system. In 1972 she was elected to the Texas House of Representatives from Harris County—the first Republican woman to serve in that body. Later, as Kay Bailey Hutchison, she served as state Treasurer, and in 1994 became the first female to represent Texas in the United States Senate. (*Houston Chronicle*)

Epilogue

Unlike a tapestry with threads of fabric, one woven with threads of history never fades, does not decay, and cannot be forgotten. The tapestry that is Houston's history is still being created, and though it—like those woven of cloth—has flaws, many of its older threads seem stronger than ever, are brighter and more vivid in color, and are more visible than in the past.

This book has attempted to show how women comprise many of the threads that have been woven into the tapestry that is the history of Houston, and how through the years those threads—once almost imperceptible—have become clearly visible throughout the tapestry.

Women of all races, creeds, and backgrounds are found today in offices and on construction sites, in theaters and space shuttles, in laboratories and classrooms, in courtrooms and emergency rooms, as police officers and firefighters, in pulpits and the armed forces, and in their more traditional but vital roles as wives and mothers. They are participants in almost every human endeavor.

This book is a celebration of their lives and an acknowledgment of their presence in the tapestry that reflects the life of our city.

The tapestry will endure, and those threads that were for so long invisible will be clearly seen by generations to come.

Astronaut Eileen Collins
(National Space and
Aeronautics Administration)

The Community House Preschool began in 1953 as a nursery. Today it is a fully accredited preschool where three-and-four-year-old children at risk are introduced to the world of academics through a professionally designed program.

Each year the Houston Junior Forum awards scholarships to high school seniors who attended the Preschool. Since 1976, the program has awarded four-year scholarships to eighty students.

The Houston Junior Forum

The Houston Junior Forum is a non-profit women's volunteer organization committed to providing charitable service to the children, youth, and senior adults in the Houston community. Established in 1946 by twenty-two women, today the Forum has over eight hundred members who give in excess of 21,000 volunteer hours yearly. Expanding from its first undertaking—organizing and staffing a library at Rusk Settlement House—the Forum now has five projects throughout the city.

For fifty-four years the Houston Junior Forum has been a source of support and service to the community. It enters the twenty-first century with renewed dedication to continue in fulfilling that mission.

The Recreation Center for Older Adults is a multi-purpose center designed to enrich the lives of senior adults through classes, lectures, field trips, and crafts. Membership is free and open to the public. The Senior Guidance Program, an information and referral service, provides assistance on issues and needs unique to senior adults and their caregivers. Its directory, filled with useful and vital information for Houston's older adult population, is published annually and distributed free throughout the community.

The Houston Junior Forum Resale Shop, established in 1969, provides low-cost and gently-used merchandise to the community while generating funds for the Forum's other projects.

Selected Bibliography

Beeth, Howard and Cary D. Wintz, ed. *Black Dixie: Afro-Texan History and Culture in Houston.* College Station: Texas A&M University Press, 1992.

Bernhard, Virginia. *Ima Hogg - The Governor's Daughter.* Austin: Texas Monthly Press, 1984.

Blackwelder, Julia Kirk. *Now Hiring: The Feminization of Work in the United States, 1900-1995.* College Station: Texas A&M University Press, 1997.

Chapman, Betty T. "From the Parlor to the Public: New Roles for Women in Houston, 1885–1918" in *The Houston Review*, Vol. XV, No. 1, 1993.

Covey, Cyclone, trans, and ed. *Cabeza de Vaca's Adventures in the Unknown Interior of America.* Albuquerque: University of New Mexico Press, 1983.

Crawford, Ann Fears. *Frankie: Mrs. R. D. Randolph and Texas Liberal Politics.* Austin: Eakin Press, 2000.

Crawford, Vicki L., Jacqueline Anne Rouse and Barbara Woods, ed. *Women in the Civil Rights Movement.* Bloomington: Indiana University Press, 1993.

Evans, Sara M. *A History of Women in America.* New York: The Free Press, 1989.

Downs, Fane and Nancy Baker Jones, ed. *Women and Texas History: Selected Essays.* Austin: Texas State Historical Association, 1993.

Exley, Jo Ella Powell, ed. *Texas Tears and Texas Sunshine: Voices of Frontier Women.* College Station: Texas A&M University Press, 1985.

Farrell, Mary D. and Elizabeth Silverthorne. *First Ladies of Texas.* Belton, Tx: Stillhouse Hollow Publishers, Inc., 1976.

Gray, Millie Richards. *The Diary of Millie Gray, 1832–1840.* Houston: Fletcher Young Publishing Company for the Rosenberg Library Press, 1967.

Hatch, Orin Walker. *Lyceum to Library: A Chapter in the Cultural History of Houston.* Houston: Texas Gulf Coast Historical Association, 1965.

Holley, Mary Austin. *The Texas Diary, 1835–1838.* Ed. James Perry Bryan. Published by the Humanities Research Center, University of Texas. Distributed by University of Texas Press, 1965.

Houghton, Dorothy Knox Howe, Barrie M. Scardino, Sadie Gwin Blackburn, and
Katherine S. Howe. *Houston's Forgotten Heritage: Landscape, Houses,
Interiors, 1824–1914*. Houston: Rice University Press, 1991.

Johnston, Marguerite. *Houston: The Unknown City*. College Station: Texas A&M
University Press, 1991.

Kerber, Linda K., Alice Kessler-Harris and Kathryn Kish Sklar. *U.S. History as Women's
History*. Chapel Hill: University of North Carolina Press, 1995.

Krenek, Thomas H. *Del Pueblo*. Houston: Houston International University, 1989.

McArthur, Judith N. *Creating the New Woman: The Rise of Southern Women's Progressive
Culture in Texas, 1893–1918*. Urbana: University of Illinois Press, 1998.

Ricklis, Robert A. *The Karankawa Indians of Texas*. Austin: University of Texas Press,
1996.

Rogers, Mary Beth. *Barbara Jordan: American Hero*. New York: Bantam Books, 1998.

Roussel, Hubert. *The Houston Symphony Orchestra 1913–1971*. Austin: University of
Texas Press, 1972.

Scott, Anne Firor. *Natural Allies, Women's Associations in American History*. Urbana:
University of Illinois Press, 1991.

Silverthorne, Elizabeth and Geneva Fulgham. *Women Pioneers in Texas Medicine*.
College Station: Texas A&M University Press, 1997.

Solomon, Barbara Miller. *In the Company of Educated Women: A History of Women and
Higher Education in America*. New Haven: Yale University Press, 1985.

Tyler, Ron, ed. *The New Handbook of Texas, Vol. 1–6*. Austin: Texas State Historical
Association, 1996.

Winegarten, Ruthe. *Black Texas Women: 150 Years of Trial and Triumph*. Austin:
University of Texas Press, 1995.

Winegarten, Ruthe and Judith N. McArthur, ed. *Citizens at Last: The Woman Suffrage
Movement in Texas*. Austin: Ellen C. Temple, 1987.

Winegarten, Ruthe. *Texas Women: A Pictorial History from Indians to Astronauts*.
Austin: Eakin Press, 1986.

Index

About the Author

Betty Trapp Chapman is a native of Tupelo, Mississippi. After graduating from Millsaps College in Jackson, Mississippi, she moved to Houston and soon immersed herself in research and study of the city and its people. She has spent much of the last twenty years teaching, lecturing, and writing with the goal of instilling in others an appreciation of Houston's past and preserving its history for future generations.

In addition to writing, "Houston Heritage," a weekly column for *Houston Business Journal*, Chapman has authored works including *Historic Houston, An Illustrated History and Resource Guide*; *2-Minute Histories of Houston*, a compilation of "Houston Heritage" articles; *Houston Then and Now*, a supplemental text for the area's elementary schools; and "From the Parlor to the Public: New Roles for Women In Houston, 1885-1918," which appeared in *The Houston Review*.

Currently listed in *Who's Who of American Women*, she has served on the boards of The Heritage Society, the Greater Houston Preservation Alliance, and the Houston Junior Forum.

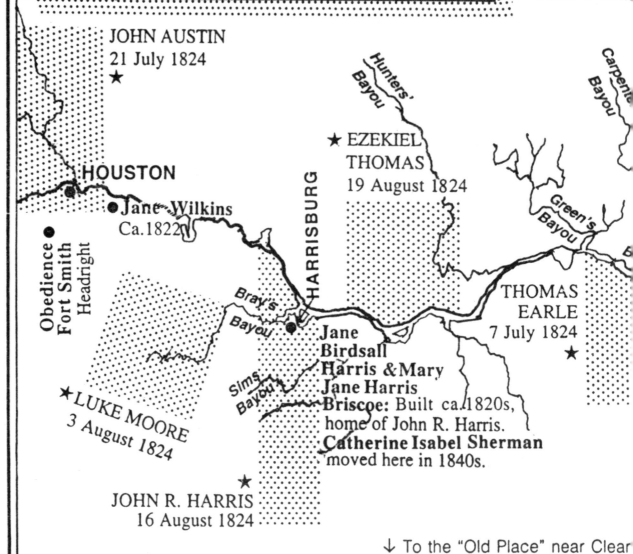

**SETTLEMENT ALONG
BUFFALO BAYOU AND THE
SAN JACINTO RIVER:
1824-1840**

● = Landmark Sites
★ = Selected 1824 Land Grants
⨯ = San Jacinto Battleground

Map by James L. Glass, 2000

NORTH

★ AMY V
16 Augu
"White's Settl

JOHN AUSTIN
21 July 1824
★

Hunters'
Bayou

★ EZEKIEL
THOMAS
19 August 1824

Carpent
Bayou

● HOUSTON

● Jane Wilkins
Ca.1822

Green's
Bayou

● Obedience Fort Smith Headright

HARRISBURG

Bray's
Bayou

THOMAS
EARLE
7 July 1824
★

Sims
Bayou

Jane
Birdsall
Harris & Mary
Jane Harris
Briscoe: Built ca.1820s,
home of John R. Harris.
Catherine Isabel Sherman
moved here in 1840s.

★ LUKE MOORE
3 August 1824

★
JOHN R. HARRIS
16 August 1824

↓ To the "Old Place" near Clear